China Catalyst

China Catalyst

Powering Global Growth by Reaching the Fastest Growing Consumer Market in the World

DAVE M. HOLLOMAN

WILEY

For general information on our other products and services or for technical support, please contact our Customer Care Department within the United States at (800) 762-2974, outside the United States at (317) 572-3993 or fax (317) 572-4002.

Wiley publishes in a variety of print and electronic formats and by print-on-demand. Some material included with standard print versions of this book may not be included in e-books or in print-on-demand. If this book refers to media such as a CD or DVD that is not included in the version you purchased, you may download this material at http://booksupport.wiley.com. For more information about Wiley products, visit www.wiley.com.

Library of Congress Cataloging-in-Publication Data:

Printed in the United States of America
Holloman, Dave M., 1969–
  China catalyst : powering global growth by reaching the fastest growing consumer markets in the world / Dave M. Holloman.
      pages cm
  Includes bibliographical references and index.
  ISBN 978-1-118-41129-2 (cloth); ISBN 978-1-118-66127-7 (ebk.);
ISBN 978-1-118-66127-7 (ebk.); ISBN 978-1-118-41770-6 (ebk.)
  1. China—Commerce. 2. China—Foreign economic relations. 3. Investments, Foreign—China. 4. International business enterprises—China. 5. Economic development—China. I. Title.
  HF3836.5.H65 2013
  382.0951—dc23
                                                                    2013005967

10 9 8 7 6 5 4 3 2 1

Contents

Preface

Reaching the Chinese consumer will be one of the defining economic and business challenges of this decade.

China's economy is in the middle of a robust transition to an economy that is rapidly becoming consumer led. This book will cover the steps companies are taking to supply the Chinese consumer and fuel their next phase of growth. Corporate leaders have realized that tapping the full growth opportunity in the Chinese market is now a competitive requirement.

Before the 2007 recession, growth in emerging markets was often viewed as an opportunity for additional leverage—something that was viewed as a "nice to have." Not anymore. Now, with U.S. consumer spending levels expected to remain low and western Europe's economic austerity projected to last years, capturing growth in the Chinese market is more important than ever. Some estimates indicate that the Chinese consumer will contribute more than a quarter of global consumption within the next 15 years.

Despite this opportunity, many companies are not yet fully equipped with the knowledge and organization to reach the Chinese consumer. Just how do you reach 1 billion consumers, anyway? The answer to that question involves a reconfiguration of many companies' approaches to the market across the full spectrum of their operations. Companies will need to transition from a primarily export-driven supply chain to a supply chain that both promotes and serves domestic demand. They will need to change their historical focus from a few regions of the country to its breadth and localize products not just for one market but for many.

It will not be easy; the journey will be full of challenges and hard choices. The purpose of this book is to outline the economic imperative, provide a baseline for the vast differences in the market, explore how the consumer market continues to evolve, and begin to outline strategies for how companies can successfully increase their market presence. The companies that successfully make this transition will be among the winners in the next phase of global growth. This new growth phase is just beginning, and this book will enable the reader to be at the forefront in understanding and taking advantage of this historic shift.

When was the last time you looked at a map of China? Do you know where the city of Chengdu is? Chengdu will have a population of more than 10 million people within 10 years or so. Do you know the difference between Sichuan and Shenzhen? The difference in income, consumer savings, the propensity to buy, and what consumers will buy is significant. In 2011–2012, the 10 fastest growing cities in the world by gross domestic product (GDP) were all in China. Beijing and Shanghai were not on the list. Instead, the 10 fastest growing cities in the world include Chongqing, Shenyang, Hefei, and Wuhan.[1] All of them lie west of China's coast, the epicenter of the country's rise onto the world's economic stage. Increasingly, these cities will be where the competitive battles for global market share will be won and lost.

The odds are that you will be looking at a map of China a lot more in the coming years. The ability to comprehend the consumer opportunity it now represents and to help claim it will be an integral part of most companies' futures. This book is designed to provide that knowledge. It will help the reader gain the insights to deliver that growth and reach the consumers who will be a driving component in the global growth engine. It will enable supply chain executives, market planners, and business strategists with more tools to operate at the forefront of this market transition.

This book is organized into three distinct parts of discovery and learning:

- Part I, "The New Phase of Global Growth," provides historical context. Chapter 1 examines how China emerged from a state of turbulence in the twentieth century to its current state of economic ascendancy. In Chapter 2, the extraordinary transition currently underway is examined in depth, demonstrating how a consumer-led economy is becoming a reality. Current industry data and research along with demographic trends form the economic imperative for companies to act with a sense of urgency. Chapter 3 outlines the catalysts driving increased market access and growth across the country.
- Part II, "Markets, Channels, and Capabilities," explores the new hot spots of demand as China's economic expansion broadens. Chapter 4 provides a fact-based geographical segmentation of the market. This segmentation helps to identify the demand hot spots and provides an example for how companies can effectively organize their strategies and operations. Chapter 5 outlines the consumer channels to market, highlighting the growth of modern retail alongside the institutions that are the legacies of a state-run economy. No survey of China's consumers can be complete without addressing the unique online world in the market. Chapter 6 provides an overview of China's digital world and

how it uniquely influences how consumers search for, buy, and consume products. Distribution capability has often been a do-it-yourself proposition in the market, and its current trends and challenges are outlined in Chapter 7. Chapter 8 provides a deep profile of a high-growth city where the next round of consumer growth is occurring.

- Part III, "Forging Ahead," provides a consolidation of market dynamics, evolution, and the future state of the retail model in the Chinese market. Chapter 9 discusses the fact that as emerging markets begin setting the global growth agenda, innovations created and proven in China will be increasingly exported abroad. China as a new center of innovation and its implications are covered in Chapter 10, and Chapter 11 provides some final thoughts on strategic options and the implications for companies seeking to reach more consumers in the market.

Throughout the book, sidebars will raise awareness about the actions that leading companies with long track records are taking to develop their markets. We will also explore how the flow of goods reaches the consumer.

In April 2012, China became the largest grocery market in the world.[2] This follows what is becoming an increasingly familiar pattern of "largest market" awards. From cars to appliances, China is becoming the largest source of current and future growth. Yet the upside and vast potential of this is just now being tapped.

As of this writing, however, gray clouds are forming once again over the global economy. Unlike the financial crisis of 2007, the current economic slowdown has China in its crosshairs as well. This book is about the future that lies beyond the horizon of immediate concerns. A new era, dominated by the Chinese consumer, is beginning to take shape. Whether the process is slowed by economic austerity or accelerated, the emergence of China's consumer economy will happen, and it is time to prepare.

I hope you find that this book deepens your understanding of the vast opportunity at hand, the challenges presented by it, and the paths to seize and capture the next phase of global growth.

Notes

1. Derek Thompson, "2012's Fastest Growing (and Shrinking) Cities," Atlantic Cities, December 1, 2012, www.theatlanticcities.com.

2. "Grocers' Green, China Overtakes America to Become the World's Largest Grocery Market," Economist, April 10, 2012, www.economist.com/blogs/graphicdetail/2012/04/daily-chart-3.

Acknowledgments

I once heard a story about a grade school boy who was very late in starting a required research report on birds. He was panicking at the amount of work he needed to accomplish at the last hours prior to the assignment's deadine. His older sister calmed him down by advising him to think about the assignment in steps. "Take it bird by bird," she said. This story, told to me as I started to write this book, is an example of the kind words and encouragement I received along the way. There are too many examples like this to count.

The vision, dedication, and perseverance it takes to finish a book is never a solo effort. It is the product of many people who encourage, review, suggest, edit, contribute, and plan. It is also the product of shared inspiration. I have been unbelievably fortunate to be affiliated with so many people in my career who have planted seeds of inspiration that ultimately led to this book. Although I cannot thank everyone who provided help along the way, certain people deserve a special note of thanks.

These thanks begin with the special folks at the Kellogg Graduate School of Management at Northwestern University. After being admitted into the university many years ago, the school has been a source of learning and pride. The professors who instructed me were the highest example of passion for the pursuit of new knowledge that continues to inspire. Dr. David Besanko, one of the brightest, committed professors anywhere, was always willing to offer advice and encouragement. Dr. Sunil Chopra welcomed me into his office to exchange ideas and provide connections to others who would help. Paul Christensen offered to review portions of the manuscript and was generous with his times and ideas. Amid a busy schedule teaching the next generation of business leaders, pushing the boundaries of research, and leading the school into new areas, each somehow found time to return my e-mails within a day, always with offers of advice and encouragement.

Fellow Kellogg alumnus Dan Frey, currently leading the China office at ZS Associates, was a wonderful source of feedback and ideas on the book.

His time and perspective working with his clients in the market proved an invaluable contribution. Sundi Aiyer, an old colleague and friend, similarly provided long e-mails full of wonderful ideas. His many years of experience working across Asia served as an excellent sounding board. A special thanks to Anita Slomski, a friend and professional writer, for her encouragement, optimism, and can-do attitude when all I could see was the long road ahead.

The staff at John Wiley & Sons was superb. The editors' patience and collaborative style moved us steadily forward to a manuscript that is no doubt much better than anything I could have written alone.

I also owe a debt of gratitude to my colleagues at IBM, whose tireless energy and unswerving dedication to clients is a reservoir that never runs dry. Kris Pederson has always, throughout my career, encouraged me to push the boundaries of current thinking into new areas. This book would not have been possible without these colleagues' many examples and encouragement throughout the years.

This book would also not have been possible without the support of my family. My wonderful wife, Shan, generously looked the other way while I was sequestered in the home office for many weekends of writing. My son, Evan, who shares a passion for the creative process, always offered "cool" as a response to any report on the current ups and downs of book research and writing. My daughter, Kacey, with her broad smile and pure, unfiltered excitement, offered more encouragement than she knows and got me back on track when I needed it.

To those listed here and to all my other friends and colleagues who listened and encouraged, thank you. Each of you helped me make a small contribution and a dream come true.

PART I

The New Phase of Global Growth

CHAPTER 1

Into the Light: China's First Economic Miracle

It is better to let half of the people die so that the other half can eat their fill.

—Chairman Mao Zedong

Past is not always prologue. Poverty can turn into prosperity. Nations and people do change for the better and progress. For China, that progress has come in the last four decades. The growing middle class across the emerging world has been led in both pace and size by China. As incomes grow, middle-class aspirations are increasingly displacing more basic concerns.

It was not always this way. In fact, China's recent history in the last 100 years has been largely defined by the quest for individual survival. China rivals any country in the world for the amount of suffering its citizens endured during the twentieth century. *Grim catastrophe* is a description that seems to vastly understate the plight of the Chinese people at points in the last century.

At the hands of both its own rulers and occupiers, China's people were catapulted through multiple chaotic periods of oppression. The twentieth century began with revolution and the downfall of emperor-led rule. The 1911 revolution overthrew the Qing dynasty, which had ruled since the year 1644. After its overthrow, regional fiefdoms emerged ruled by warlords. China changed its head of state 6 times and its prime minister 22 times between 1917 and 1928.[1] During the same time frame, hundreds of mutinies and interprovincial wars occurred. Anarchy often prevailed: whoever controlled the local army at any given time ruled the day. The stability of the country suffered.

The Kuomintang Party emerged to unify the country. By 1928, its armies fought their way to make it the recognized governing party of the country. Officially, the country had become unified. In reality, many factions of the warlord period remained and were stoked by another emerging force: the Communist Party of China. Founded in Shanghai in 1921 and supported by the new Soviet regime, the Communists challenged the Kuomintang's authority from the start. Ethnic rebellions started to occur as well. Banditry filled the vacuum created by the inability to implement the rule of law.

In response, the Kuomintang fed its totalitarian tendencies and cracked down hard. Self-labeled as the Nationalists, the Kuomintang developed a reputation for iron-fisted tactics and fascist rule. The Communists pushed back and moved the country yet again toward war. The darkness of warlord anarchy, replaced by totalitarian rule, was then followed by the prospect and onset of civil war.

Enter Japan. The Japanese ended the escalation toward civil war as they began their invasion and occupation throughout Asia. They added to the bloodshed and misery through their ruthless occupation of China during World War II. Their atrocities have been well documented: the Japanese army raped and pillaged its way across much of the country, perpetrating the mass murder of 4 million Chinese.

At the end of World War II, warlord rule, civil war, and foreign occupation had taken its toll on China. About 10 million Chinese had died fighting the Japanese occupation. In the years immediately after World War II, another 5 million died in a struggle to determine the country's rulers. Chiang Kai-shek and his authoritarian Kuomintang Party were chased to the island of Taiwan as the Communists prevailed, taking power in 1949.

Within the first 50 years of the twentieth century, more than 20 million Chinese had died prematurely. After so much carnage, the peasant army seized control and announced a strong, unified nation that would put the people in charge. The governing party promised to be the instrument for China's march toward an Eden of prosperity. It was, for the foreseeable future, not to be.

What followed was bloodier still. The proposed paradise soon turned into inescapable evil for China's inhabitants. Mao's fight for power over the next few decades ultimately destroyed the country's institutions and decimated the elements of civil society. Millions starved in one of the greatest famines ever known. Families were separated. People were beaten, tortured, and killed in untold numbers. The country spiraled into lawlessness and economic decline.

In the years immediately after the Communist revolution, Chairman Mao became determined to overtake the Soviet Union as the world's preeminent communist power. Mao had relied on Joseph Stalin and the Soviets for years for aid to his army. The quid pro quo for this aid was Soviet influence on the tactics and strategy Mao was pursuing. All too often, Mao thought he had to placate the Soviets. He finally became tired of playing the perceived second fiddle and saw the opportunity to lead the push toward a communist-dominated world.

But progress was slow in China. The early efforts to collectivize society met with meager results. The moderate elements within the Communist Party called for a more gradual and mixed path toward a centralized economy. But Mao's ambition continued to burn, and he viewed challenges to his economic plans as threats to his seat of power. He began purging those he viewed as threats from the party ranks. Any subordinate who offered anything other than unflinching support and admiration was labeled a "rightist." Having this label stick meant the end of one's political career, political exile, and no options. Fearing for their jobs, Mao's lieutenants provided unswerving support, delivered as worship, of the country's leader.

Mao was determined to prove the communist model superior to Western capitalism, so he promised to overtake Britain in the industrial output of steel in a few years. His plan called for implementing radical changes down to the lowest levels of society. The country's citizens would be organized into one large, unified labor force. In the countryside, all aspects of farming would be collectivized. Individual lands would be confiscated to form large agricultural communes. People in the cities would be mobilized into industry. Large grand designs to dam and redirect rivers would be initiated to tap the power of nature and lead to newfound gains in energy and output.

Raising grain output was the linchpin of the strategy. Surplus grain output would feed the urban industrial workforce and would also be exported. Large volumes of grain would be sold to pay off the country's debt, which was viewed as a sign of dependency that should quickly be shed. Selling grain would also fund the central planning goal of building up the country's steel industry. Most important, surplus grain would serve as a beacon to the world, signaling the country's growing vitality and the superiority of the communist system. Grain output would be the litmus test of success.

Beginning in the late 1950s, Chairman Mao called for a plan he dubbed the Great Leap Forward to implement these strategies. The nation was militarized. Army uniforms became the regular dress. Kitchens were collectivized. Backyard furnaces were built to burn scrap metal in service to the state plan. Everyone carried their pots and pans to government collection points to be melted into steel. After that, people ate at the pleasure of the state, based on the government's definition of merit. A revolution had begun, but it would soon turn into horror.

A System Spirals Out of Control

Fear of persecution drove the country into a downward spiral. The initial months of the campaign filled Chairman Mao with increasing enthusiasm. Provinces kept reporting grain yields that exceeded the planned targets. Mao was overjoyed. A confident Mao boasted that the country would not know what to do with all of its excess grain. And much of the world believed it. Visiting dignitaries were taken to show villages, token communes full of happy workers producing a world full of joy and abundance.

In reality, mass starvation was beginning to take root. The reports of grain yields surpassing planned targets continued to be inflated as severe punishments were meted out to the provinces that failed to reach their assigned targets. The practice became rampant at every level in the reporting chain. The central government took its allotted amount, which continued to increase, and funneled it to the urban areas and for export, leaving little for the rural laborers to consume.

Yet the output targets kept increasing. Faced with the fear of their own persecution, government officials escalated the harsh treatment of rural workers, determined to reach ever-rising targets with fewer resources. People forced into labor were eating less and working more in the harshest of conditions. As food production continued to plummet, starvation became a decision made by the government officials in the field. Women, children, and the elderly were often fed last, since they were either unable to work or less productive. Those who did not pull their weight or who fell out of favor were denied food. When the food ran out, the citizens were left to forage, feeding on roots and mud to stay alive.

China's landscape became barren. People's homes were torn down to feed the backyard furnaces designed to boost steel production. Anything melted in the furnaces was largely useless for producing industrial-grade steel, but targets and the threat of persecution drove collective madness. Any structure that could burn was burned, and anything that could be melted went into the furnace. Those who resisted were tortured. Imagine a group of people working under armed guard across a barren landscape, and you will start to grasp the desolation unfolding across China during this time. There were no houses; they had been torn down and burned. There were no trees. There was only the promise of gruel coming from work and unswerving obedience. Chaos set in.

After nearly four years, as the evidence finally came to light, the Great Leap Forward came to an end. Current estimates suggest that more than 45 million people died in four years from unnatural causes. Most died in the famine. Millions died in the struggles that preceded the mass starvation, including through suicide and torture. "It is impossible not to beat people to death," a county leader said during the campaign.

The true size of the catastrophe would remain unknown to the world for decades, and it still remains little-known relative to the other great famines and genocides of comparable size in world history. It was not until the late 1990s that accounts and facts began to surface suggesting the massive scale of the disaster. Even today, there is no recognition or trace of the Great Leap Forward in China. The government denies many of the facts; it admits that a famine occurred but says it was caused by natural forces.

The Great Leap Forward is a ghost, but a young one. Only 60 years old, this and the other campaigns have left a shadow over the country, and many wonder whether the nation has fully come to grips with its recent tragic history.[2]

Chaos Returns

After the Great Leap Forward's disastrous results, Chairman Mao was challenged by moderates in the governing Communist Party, who emerged to take a more prominent role in determining the country's economic direction. Simultaneously, Mao began laying the groundwork for "continuous revolution," which would ultimately lead the country back into chaos. Fearing his continued political vulnerability, Mao worked to reestablish his power base in the years after the Great Leap Forward.

Quietly, he purged his enemies from the governing ranks and laid the foundation for a political campaign that would once again give rise to his absolute power. He did so by enlisting the country's youth in loose organizations that became known as the Red Guards. This political campaign, starting in 1966 and lasting through 1976, became known as the Cultural Revolution. Universities closed and industry shut down as millions were sent to the countryside for "education through labor."

The Red Guards became increasingly empowered and accountable to no one. Their passion was used to bully and abuse those who threatened the chairman's power. The Red Guards set about destroying the country's cultural relics that competed with the philosophical primacy of communism. Those who were branded as "bourgeois" or "intellectuals"—basically, anyone with more than a middle school education or a background that suggested anything other than total allegiance to the Communist Party—could be, and were, targeted for brutal public harassment and reeducation in the labor camps.

The nation was turned upside down, with its citizens more concerned again about daily survival than the pursuit of any kind of standard of living associated with the modern world. With a 1966 dictate from Mao prohibiting the police from intervening in Red Guard actions, society descended into lawlessness. Chairman Mao's death in 1976 closed the chapter on this awful period. Persecuted moderates reestablished their power and began to pick up the pieces of a broken society.[3]

Once the nation started rebuilding itself, it did so under the economic and governing control of the state-run, Stalinist model. People's housing was controlled by their employers, who administered almost every aspect of people's lives. This was referred to at the time by the Chinese term *dan wei*, which means "work unit." This economic structure, composed of the central planning of industry down to the day-to-day administration of the workers, ensured a draconian control of party doctrine. For example, the requirement that Chinese citizens obtain the permission of their state-run employers to marry officially ended only in 2003.

Outside working hours, individual lives were watched closely by street committees. The head of each local street committee lived in an apartment provided by the government. A network of informers updated the head of the street committee about people's whereabouts. These informers knew who received visitors. Apartment inspections were instigated at a moment's notice, on a whim, without any oversight. The street committee granted the right of a married couple to have a family.

Political sessions were yet another element of the state-designed system of control, and they were usually dominated by coercion and mental abuse. There was no escaping the prying eyes of the state. Perceived violations, which could happen simply by falling out of favor with the head of one's street committee or work unit supervisor, could mean imprisonment, coercion, bad work assignments, and family separations through work assignments.

These times of political campaigns and political control gave way to the modern rise of *guan xi*. The Chinese concept of *guan xi* has been written about extensively. In recent years, it has often been presented as a gateway to understanding Chinese culture and an insight to doing business in the country. Loosely translated as "connections" and "relationships," *guan xi* is a central organizing premise of Chinese culture. Its cultural understanding is deep, and it taps into a system of personal connections that is the lubricant of Chinese society. Before it became fashionable, *guan xi's* practice formed an underground economy that enabled people to survive through favor and exchange in such a draconian system and a society marked by scarcity. In those days, currency was not widely available, and a barter economy developed. Usually, what was bartered was access to scarce resources or influence within the control apparatus of the state.

The oppressive implementation of Mao's political campaigns virtually eliminated the consumer economy. In 1957, just before the launch of the Great Leap Forward, about 1 million retail outlets existed in the country. By 1981, at the close of the Great Leap Forward and the Cultural Revolution, the number of stores had shrunk to 190,000. At the same time, China's population had increased from 600 million to 1 billion. In the capital city, the number of restaurants had plummeted from more than 10,000 to fewer than 700.[4]

Life had turned dark. The Communist regime's emphasis on heavy industry through central planning gutted the consumer market. Scarcity was rampant across all categories, which resulted in the rationing of consumer goods like food, furniture, and housing. The practice of using connections became a substitute for a just and equitable system in a society of scarcity. Though unwritten, it became the primary organizing premise of society. Things like marriage approvals, work unit assignments, and housing all operated in politicized, bureaucratic structures. Generations of favor exchanges between people were called on to inject personal connections into these structures. All the practical considerations of life were accomplished by subverting the current system through personal connections that enabled one to go "through the back door."[5]

A country in economic tatters was what moderate Communist Party member Deng Xiaoping inherited after his reemergence as a party leader at the end of the Cultural Revolution. In the generation that endured the Great Leap Forward and the Cultural Revolution, the economic results reveal the tragedy of lost time and ruined lives. During the two decades of political campaigns, the standard of living for urban citizens stagnated. Rural citizens' standard of living remained at the same level as in the 1930s.

As other Asian countries, such as Japan and South Korea, emerged in the late 1970s with thriving economies, China remained economically static and poor. The nation's economic infrastructure was also splintered. After years of neglect of education, illiteracy was rampant; some estimates are that 45 percent of the population was illiterate. The collectivization of agriculture had resulted in a food supply insufficient to meet the needs of the country.

Figure 1.1 outlines the economic contraction during the two political campaigns. In the years preceding the death of Mao Zedong, the influences driving the chaos of the Cultural Revolution waned, moderates like Deng Xiaoping were restored to power, and a more rapid pace of economic growth began. As the era of political campaigns ended and reform began, China's economy, despite the country's great size and resources, was roughly only the size of Italy's.

This backdrop and economic inheritance drove Deng's actions as he took the reins of power. Starting in 1978, Deng unfurled a set of economic reforms that laid the foundation for dramatic change. This included the privatization of agriculture, the legalization of private enterprise, the loosening of the production of state-run firms from government-imposed quotas, and invitations to foreign investors. "Socialism does not mean shared poverty," he once said.[6]

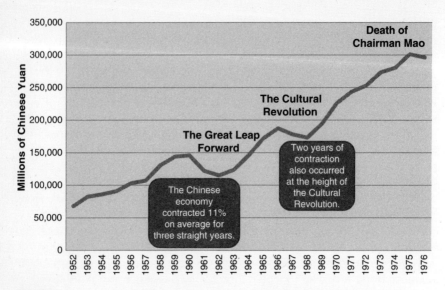

FIGURE 1.1 People's Republic of China, Gross Domestic Product (1952–1976)

Chief among these new reforms was the establishment of special areas to be exempted from the oppressive state-run control that ruled the rest of the nation. The Special Economic Zones, as they were named, were a bold experiment to complement and add urgency to country-wide reforms. The reforms were dramatic, with most of the established zones in the southern coastal parts of the country. The Special Economic Zones were established and guided by key principles articulated into law. These included a primary focus on export, incentives to attract foreign capital for construction, and greater autonomy from top-down, centralized planning.

The Chinese Communists had always held economic self-sufficiency as a chief goal. It was a core belief that became a national mission in order to demonstrate the supremacy of the communist ideology and not be seen as dependent on capitalist economies. Enactment of the Special Economic Zones eschewed this national policy of economic self-reliance by encouraging and embracing the need for foreign investment. The Special Economic Zones became an economic laboratory in which the results could be scaled and leveraged for political gain and further reform.

As the end of the 1980s approached, Deng's ambitious experiment appeared to be yielding results. China seemed poised to emerge from the dark days of the past and raise its people higher on the economic ladder.

Then the Tiananmen Square uprising occurred in June 1989. In 1989, the Soviet Union was experiencing glasnost and would ultimately disintegrate. A wave of people power was starting to unfold across Eastern Europe as the shackles of post–World War II communism were loosened.

In November 1989, the Berlin Wall came down, and East Berlin was once again reunited with its western sibling.

Meanwhile, China's own brand of political change was brewing. Responding to rising inflation and concerns of widespread corruption, a small, elite class of students from Peking University, the most prestigious university in China, started a protest in Tiananmen Square. Aimed at the very heart of China's governing party, the protests would grow and be broadcast around the world. The world media had been sent to cover the state visit by Soviet premier Mikhail Gorbachev, but they turned their cameras instead onto the masses of students populating the central square of the country in protest.

Although a few moderates within the ruling class supported the students in their calls for reform, the more influential hard-liners embraced a confrontational stance as the protests grew. Ultimately, the order was given for tanks to roll in and crush the movement. It's impossible to estimate just how close the students' efforts came to making their calls for reform a success. On what seemed like the precipice of real change and victory, a long night of shooting and violence crushed the students' hopes.

History has noted that China came close to either real change or chaos. With recent history ever present in the minds of the Chinese leadership, protests like the Tiananmen Square uprising are often viewed through the lens of being instigators of chaos. The merits of the cause and compromise often take a backseat, and Tiananmen Square especially raised concerns of destabilization and civil strife. The long shadow of China's recent past reared its head again as the calls for reform met with resistance steeped in fear of a return to chaos.

The economic repercussions of the Tiananmen Square protests were swift. Many multinational corporations that had initially embraced economic reform left China, concerned about the reputational effects of appearing to support the government crackdown. China faced the prospect of international rebuke and economic boycott. Many of the young, educated elite in the country decided to take advantage of loosening immigration policies in the United States and elsewhere to emigrate from China. This resulted in a drought of human capital.

Perhaps the greatest threat to continued economic reform was within the ruling Communist Party itself. Through the authoritarian crackdown, hard-liners steeped in communist orthodoxy reemerged to challenge the more moderate, reform-minded wing of the party. Party officials who supported calls for more aggressive reform were purged after the crackdown. A prominent supporter and ally of Deng, Zhao Ziyang, was excommunicated and put under house arrest. This sentence persisted until his death in 2005. An 18-month period of retrenchment and unease followed the crackdown. Now retired from his official government posts, Deng searched for a way to reignite his reform agenda.

Riding South to Reignite Reform

During the early part of 1992, with his ability to implement further economic reforms at risk, Deng rode a train south from Beijing to the established Special Economic Zones that embodied his hope for economic progress. Twenty years earlier, Deng had been forced from his political governing position and sent to work in a factory far away from the levers of power. At odds with Chairman Mao on economic policy, Deng and his family were persecuted and excommunicated from power.

The personal cost was high. Deng spent four years doing hard labor in a tractor factory in the far western region of China. His eldest son was tortured and became a paraplegic after either jumping or being thrown from a fourth-story window. Deng revitalized his political reputation and returned to power in 1974 as first vice premier, running the government's daily affairs. Taking stock of his country's economic health proved sobering. Deng needed a response to the resistance in order for more progressive economic reforms to progress.

And so, in the beginning of 1992, Deng rode south. He decided, as past Chinese political leaders had done, to take his case directly to the public. It is a deep irony of Chinese politics that political leaders in a dictatorial, one-party system whose power is threatened have often taken their cases directly to the people to build support from the bottom up.

Change always seems to happen in the south for China. It was the southern coastal city of Shanghai that gave rise to the Communist revolution that Deng helped to lead. Deng first visited Shenzhen and other coastal cities that formed a central point in the economic experiment embodied by the Special Economic Zones. The Southern Tour, as his trip was billed, finished in Shanghai, where a relatively recent economic zone was established in the now legendary Pu Dong district.[7] The formation of the Pu Dong district, just across the river from Shanghai's center, accompanied the reopening of the Shanghai Stock Exchange, which had been shut down for 40 years since the 1949 revolution.

Deng's visit, speeches, and meetings with government officials were enthusiastically covered by the local press. With a loud voice, the press called for continued, ambitious economic reform. Yet the tour was barely mentioned in the national press, and little notice was given by the governing party in Beijing. Strong local support and Deng's remaining political influence, however, translated into continued reform executed by President Jiang Zemin. A new emerging class of ruling politicians emerged from the south, steeped in the school of economic reform. Deng's ally Zhu Rongji, whose political rise happened in the reform-minded south as Shanghai's mayor, moved up into the national governing sphere during this time as vice premier.

Resilience took root. Throughout the primacy of his political life, Deng had faced challenge, exile, persecution, and then restoration. Throughout, he remained steadfast to his economic vision of a more open and prosperous country. Deng turned his back on the chaotic political campaigns of the past that had upended the country from one extreme goal to the next, instead favoring pragmatic, progressive steps. To him and his allies, reform was the path to revolution.

The Rise of Shenzhen and a New China

Nowhere were the effects of Deng's economic reforms felt more than in the city of Shenzhen. In the early 1980s, a full decade before Deng's Southern Tour, when the Special Economic Zones were established, Shenzhen was a small fishing village. There were no paved roads to speak of, no tall buildings outlining an urban landscape, and certainly no markings of large economic commerce. Although Shenzhen sat right across the river from Hong Kong, the two locales were a world apart and completely disconnected.[8]

In the time just before economic reform, approximately 30,000 people resided in Shenzhen.[9] Today, more people are employed at one factory there than lived in the entire city before economic reform. That factory, owned by the increasingly well-known Foxconn Company, is home to more than 400,000 workers.[10] If you own an iPad, there are strong odds it was made in Shenzhen.

Shenzhen has indeed become a central point in the country's amazing economic transformation. From a population of 30,000 at the start of economic reform, the city has grown to more than 10 million in just 30 years. Today, an urban landscape rivaling any in the world rises from the ground where there were only farm fields 25 years ago. Shenzhen is home to a sprawling, modern skyline that includes the eighth tallest building in the world. In just one generation, Shenzhen's GDP has increased to nearly 1 trillion yuan annually (about $150 billion). Shenzhen is now the fifth largest urban economy in China, a major manufacturing center and home of high technology in China.

Shenzhen represents the realization of the original goals of China's economic transformation. Shenzhen is the largest export market in China, with exports contributing more than half of its GDP. This export market has been largely built by foreign investment. Between 2001 and 2010, nonfinancial foreign direct investment averaged $70 billion annually.[11] Most of that investment went into the ground in places like Shenzhen. Total foreign direct investment shows an even more striking picture, growing to $125 billion in 2010 from $7 billion in 1992.[12]

Shenzhen is a city populated through immigration. More than 80 percent of its 10 million residents are migrant workers, predominantly young people with limited education who have migrated to the coast from inland China in search of work.[13] In 1980, farmers in nearby provinces lived on an income of less than $2 per day. On the heels of the previous generation's instability, the pull of rising incomes and the stable work found in coastal factories resulted in the largest internal migration in the history of the world. Since 1978, many Chinese from these rural provinces left their homes and migrated to places like Shenzhen, and this migration grew stronger as the economy grew. Nearly 160 million people migrated from rural inland China to find work in the factories of coastal China. This migration powered the country's emerging manufacturing engine, contributing to 20 percent of China's GDP growth.[14]

The economic reforms that started more than 30 years ago initiated the rapid growth of China's new economy. Since the reforms were initiated, China's GDP has grown by an annual average of more than 15 percent. According to data from the International Monetary Fund, China has risen to become the second largest economy in the world, from fifth in 2005 and eighth in 1995.[15] Along the way, the size of China's economy eclipsed Italy, France, Britain, Germany, and Japan.

Figure 1.2 illustrates the dramatic growth experienced by the Chinese economy beginning in the 1990s.

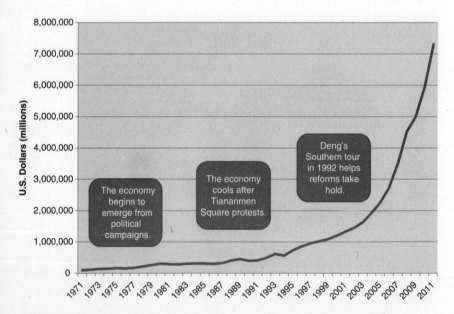

FIGURE 1.2 People's Republic of China, Gross Domestic Product (1971–2011)

Out of the darkness of China's past, the policies of economic reform catapulted the nation onto the world stage of global commerce. The successful formula underlying that transformation comprised a focus on an export-driven economy fueled by foreign investment and powered by low-cost migrant labor on an unprecedented scale. Millions of people were lifted from destitute poverty as a result.

Now every part of that formula is about to change.

Notes

1. R. J. Rummel, *China's Bloody Century: Genocide and Mass Murder since 1900* (Piscataway, NJ: Transaction, 1991).

2. The general background on the Great Leap Forward has been taken from the following sources: Frank Dikötter, *Mao's Great Famine: The History of China's Most Devastating Catastrophe, 1958–1962* (New York: Walker, 2010); Michael Fathers, "Book Review: *Tombstone: The Great Famine in China*," *Wall Street Journal*, October 26, 2012, www.wsj.com; and Jonathan Fenby, "Mao's Great Famine by Frank Dikötter," *Guardian*, September 4, 2010 www.guardian.co.uk/books/2010/sep/05/maos-great-famine-dikotter-review.

3. Roderick MacFarquhar and Michael Schoenhals, *Mao's Last Revolution* (Cambridge, MA: Harvard University Press, 2006).

4. Fox Butterfield, *China: Alive in the Bitter Sea* (New York: Times Books, 1982). Fox Butterfield was the Beijing bureau chief for the *New York Times* starting in 1979, and he was the first journalist from the *Times* to have been stationed in China in more than 30 years. This book, which won the National Book Award for Nonfiction in 1983, chronicles the story of the nation and its individuals during the aftermath of the Cultural Revolution.

5. Ibid., pp. 89–112.

6. Afshin Molavi. "The chosen few?" *National*, April 24, 2008, www.thenational.ae/arts-culture/books/the-chosen-few.

7. "Deng Xiaoping's South China Tour," April 19, 2011, China.org.cn, www.china.org.cn/archive/2011-04/19/content_22392494.htm.

8. For a fascinating set of photographs showing Shenzhen's dramatic transformation, see www.skyscrapercity.com/showthread.php?t=371989.

9. Xiangming Chen, "Magic and Myth of Migration: A Case Study of a Special Economic Zone in China," *Asia-Pacific Population Journal*, 2, no. 3, www.uic.edu/depts/soci/xmchen/APPJ_shenzhen.pdf.

10. Austin Ramzy, "Chinese Factory under Scrutiny As Suicides Mount, *Time*, May 26, 2010, www.time.com/time/world/article/0,8599,1991620,00.html.

11. U.S.-China Business Council, Foreign Direct Investment in China, www.uschina
.org/statistics/fdi_cumulative.html.

12. Google, "Public Data," www.google.com/publicdata/directory?hl=en&dl=en.

13. "A Work in Progress," *Economist*, March 17, 2011.

14. "The Largest Migration in History," *Economist* video, February 22, 2012,
www.economist.com/node/21548111. There are two wonderful sources that
examine the lives of migrant workers in China: Leslie T. Chang, *Factory Girls:
From Village to City in a Changing China* (City: Spiegel & Grau, 2009); and
Lixin Fan, dir., and Daniel Cross and Mila Aung-Thwin, prod., *Last Train Home*
(Montreal: EyeSteel Film, 2009).

15. United Nations, "National Accounts Main Database," http://unstats.un.org/unsd/
snaama/dnllist.asp.

CHAPTER 2

Economic Transition

When people say, as they often do, that "China is changing fast," they typically are referring to the country's astonishing speed of development. They point to the skyscraper-a-day building pace, cities rapidly emerging from fields, and highways seemingly appearing out of nowhere. To be sure, there are no signs that these things are going away anytime soon.

Since the mid-1980s, when economic reform started, and to a much greater extent starting in the mid-1990s, the basic formula and system for economic growth has remained the same. Low-cost labor, rural migration, a focus on export markets, and an influx of foreign investment were the key ingredients of the economic growth explosion. The system is now changing as societal trends challenge the historical growth model. Economic and demographic trends are instigating change that will bring the export-driven machine to an end as the country's driving growth engine.

These changes are highlighted in Figure 2.1 and are compared side by side with the ingredients of the China growth miracle of the last two decades.

Rising wage rates, decreasing export demand, and internal demographic changes are all sources of the change to come.

Wage Rates Are Increasing Significantly

China's economic miracle depended heavily on an abundance of cheap labor. In cities like Shenzhen, low–capital intensive, low-wage labor was abundantly supplied. Throughout the early era's surging growth in the southern provinces, wage-rate growth was far more muted and gradual than corresponding growth rates. An endless supply of workers kept coming through rural migration, and that kept workers' wages low. But labor shortages in the high-paced Special Economic Zones (SEZs) began to appear as early as 2003, which started to translate into higher wage growth. The East

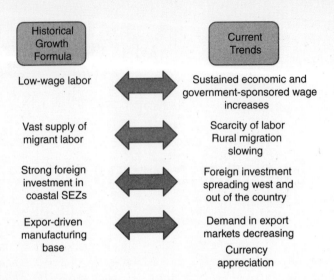

FIGURE 2.1 Trends Driving a New Economic Landscape

Asia Forum reports that manufacturing wages between 2003 and 2008 grew slightly more than 10 percent per year. In 2010, that growth rate increased to 19 percent for migrant workers. Labor shortages continue.[1] These shortages are growing deeper and lasting longer.[2] Help-wanted ads dot the landscape of the SEZs these days.

The Foxconn Company is a good example. Owned by Taiwan's Hon Hai Precision Industry Company, Foxconn has become an integral part of the global high-technology supply chain. The company makes iPads, Dell computers, and Hewlett-Packard computers. Its original factory in China is located in Shenzhen and was referred to in Chapter 1. With more than 400,000 workers on the payroll in Shenzhen alone, that work site seems more like a city than a place of employment. Dormitories house the workers. Cafeterias feed them. The Foxconn factory is both home and workplace for the vast majority of its migrant workforce. In many ways, it is a similar setup to the *dan wei* system perpetuated in China during the Mao era.

Instead of a system designed to implement party control, however, today's system is designed to generate maximum productivity at a very low cost. There are many reasons to believe that the system at Foxconn is under pressure. Reacting to a string of suicides and numerous reports of poor working conditions, the Foxconn Company has increased wage rates dramatically and on numerous occasions between 2010 and 2012. This included at least two pay raises, of 30 percent and then 66 percent, in 2010.[3] In early 2012, the company reported additional wage raises between 16 and 25 percent.[4] Foxconn's experience hints at the possibility that wage growth in the hotbed of the manufacturing SEZs is actually much higher than some reports suggest and certainly higher than the often reported country average.

Evidence also suggests that many migrant workers are not compensated for overtime hours. The concept of compensating workers for overtime was a foreign one in the early days, as the SEZs were established and grew. As these working conditions come to light, it's clear that at least in some cases, the companies that contract with these manufacturers can suffer damage to their reputations. As pressure builds to correct this, the result will most likely be continued higher wage growth.

The gap between China's wage rates and other export manufacturing centers is growing as wages continue to rise. Figure 2.2 shows how the growth in average wage rates for China has resulted in a large wage gap compared with a few alternative countries used for low-cost labor and export manufacturing. Using 2010 data, this chart shows that wage rates in China are almost four times those of Bangladesh and twice those of India and neighboring Vietnam.[5] This chart indicates that once labor scarcities started to take hold, wage rates for Chinese workers increased more and created a larger wage gap between China and other export-directed economies in the region.[6] This has resulted in many companies, including the influential and large Li & Fung, migrating more of their high-labor content manufacturing to other countries.[7] Textile exports rose 43 percent in the 12 months preceding July 2011.[8]

Wages in China are increasing to the extent that a recent study by the Boston Consulting Group suggests that the gap for high labor and highly skilled manufacturing may be closing even with the United States. The study suggests that net labor costs in the high-cost export manufacturing areas of China will converge with labor rates in some parts of the United States by 2015, accounting for the higher U.S. worker productivity.[9]

Under current conditions, China's export manufacturing base may be getting caught in a tightening squeeze, as shown in Figure 2.3. On one end,

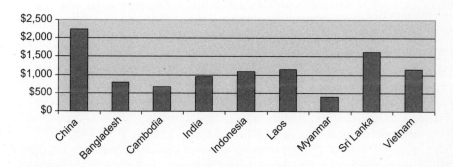

FIGURE 2.2 Comparison of Average Annual Wage Rates[10]

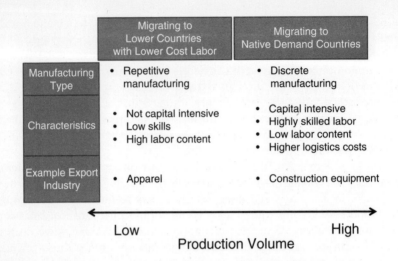

	Migrating to Lower Countries with Lower Cost Labor	Migrating to Native Demand Countries
Manufacturing Type	• Repetitive manufacturing	• Discrete manufacturing
Characteristics	• Not capital intensive • Low skills • High labor content	• Capital intensive • Highly skilled labor • Low labor content • Higher logistics costs
Example Export Industry	• Apparel	• Construction equipment

Low   High
Production Volume

FIGURE 2.3 The Labor Squeeze in China's Export Manufacturing Base

highly labor-intensive but low-skilled and low–capital intensive production will exit to lower-cost countries as the wage gap grows. On the other end, the more highly skilled, capital-intensive manufacturing base—at least a portion of it—may be imported back into the United States.

Chinese workers' wages will continue to rise. Economic changes will be spurred as wages in the hot export manufacturing areas of the coast and megacities increase.

Foreign Direct Investment Is Evolving

Since the onset of the 2009 global recession, it's no surprise that China has struggled to maintain the levels of foreign direct investment to further propel growth. In the beginning months of 2012, foreign direct investment shrank as European Union investments contracted.[11]

If and when foreign investment growth returns, it will most likely take a different form from the investment before the global economic crisis.

In China's latest five-year plan, issued in 2011, the government provided guidelines for foreign direct investment. These guidelines encouraged foreign investments in low-wage, labor-intensive industries only in the western interior of the country. Higher value-added manufacturing and supporting investments were encouraged in the economic hotbed of the south.

Clearly, the government is trying to avoid the economic labor squeeze by incentivizing its embedded manufacturing base in the south to transition into higher-level industries. Simultaneously, the government appears to be incentivizing a migration of lower-level industries into the less economically developed west.

Export-Directed Growth Is Being Challenged

In terms of absolute numbers, China's export engine is running hard. From 1992, when exports were negligible by today's standard, China's total exports expanded to more than $150 billion, accounting for approximately 40 percent of its total GDP.[12] Yet challenges exist to maintain these levels and sustain the huge growth rates underlying them.

The United States and the European Union are currently China's top two export markets. It's widely accepted that high levels of consumer consumption in the United States contributed mightily to China's economic miracle. Demand in these markets has, of course, changed dramatically since the global recession in 2009. Consumer spending in the United States has yet to fully recover, and the European Union, recovering from deep financial challenges from member nations like Greece and Spain, is poised for contraction or moderate growth at best in the foreseeable future. In short, the demand in China's largest export markets is fading.

As new global realities set in, the Chinese government is putting more resources into establishing relationships with more developing economies. China is investing significantly in its relationships throughout both the Middle East and Africa as a way to ensure access to energy supplies and also broaden the destinations of its export industries.

Happening simultaneously with declining demand is the appreciation of the Chinese currency. An appreciating currency raises the prices of China's manufactured goods in its receiving import countries. China's management of its currency continues to be the topic of a long-running, international debate. Because the Chinese central bank sets the conversion rate, other countries have expressed criticism of the policy. They suggest that the currency is set at artificially low rates and at a lower value than if the currency's conversion rate were set on the open market. Critics suggest that an artificially low currency results in artificially low export prices, in effect subsidizing the continued viability of China's export manufacturing base.

As countries and central banks debate, the value of the Chinese yuan has continued to appreciate through inflation. Continued appreciation of the yuan, combined with the significant wage increases, will make export costs climb and make the business case less compelling for China's use as an export base.

All of these trends interact to mitigate China's export growth model. The low-cost labor used in SEZ-located factories has grown scarce, driving wages up. The foreign investment used to fund those factories is decreasing and being redirected. The products made in these factories are becoming more expensive for their primary markets, where consumption is moderating.

In addition to these trends, two changes within Chinese society are pushing against the export-driven growth formula. The country is growing older, more educated, and more urban.

Demographic Megatrends

The growing age of the population is a key issue facing China. The generation of young migrant labor that enabled the economic miracle is growing older, and there is no one-for-one replacement by the younger generation. The largest contributor to the increase in age in the overall population is China's one-child policy, begun in 1979. As the country emerged from the era of political campaigns, and before the glimmers of hope that were delivered through economic reform, widespread concerns existed about the country's ability to support a growing population. Still holding on to the economic principle of self-sufficiency, the risk of experiencing another famine loomed large and resulted in the policy allowing only one child per family. Fertility rates dropped as this policy was enacted, from more than five births per woman in 1970 to just more than two in 1990. Data show that the rate has continued to drop in the most recent decade (see Figure 2.4).[13]

Declining fertility rates combined with an aging population have led to significant declines in the population share of working-age adults in what many describe as a looming crisis for the country. That trend will continue as long as the declining fertility rate holds. By 2050, China's workforce will contract by 11 percent in terms of its share of the broader population. Even then, with an average forecasted age close to 50, there will be an aging

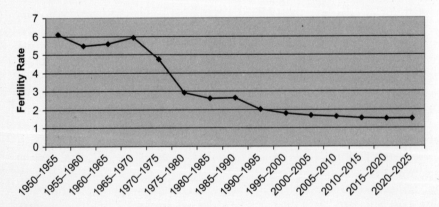

FIGURE 2.4 China's Declining Fertility Rate
Source: United Nations

workforce. The number of people entering the workforce in their 20s will be cut in half, from 120 million in 2010 to just over 60 million.[14] The generation that migrated to the factories that powered the country's export model has gotten older, with fewer workers coming in to replace those individuals.

Another key trend affecting the export-led growth model is the rising levels of education. China suffered from a "lost generation" because of the era of the political campaigns. The Cultural Revolution severely limited much of the country's education for many years as primary schools and institutions of higher education shut their doors. In the decades since, China's primary and secondary education has blossomed. Student enrollment in postsecondary education increased by a factor of 5 between the years 1997 and 2005, increasing from just over 3 million students to more than 15 million.[15] These institutions are producing more than 6 million graduates per year and are growing.[16] Yet much has been made of the unemployment rate for new graduates. Not fully industrialized, the historical low-skilled export model is unable to absorb these new graduates into the economy, which is another reason the central government is supporting the move to higher-skilled industries.

The largest trend driving change in China today is the rapid rate of urbanization across the country. In 1950, merely 13 percent of the Chinese lived in urban areas.[17] Society was, at that time, primarily agricultural and rural. Today's millions are either moving to cities seeking opportunity or being swallowed up as cities expand. In early 2012, more people in China lived in cities than in rural areas, with the urban population exceeding 690 million.[18]

McKinsey & Company estimates there will be 1 billion urban residents in China by 2030. This will include 8 cities each with a population greater than 10 million. Two of them will each have a population greater than 20 million. With those cities included, about 140 cities will each have a population greater than 1.5 million. Thus, 400 cities will each have a middle-class population greater than 250,000. By comparison, today the United States and Canada combined have 70 cities each with a middle-class population of 250,000.[19]

The world at large is becoming urban, and China will lead the way. Based on data projections from a population study conducted by the United Nations, Figure 2.5 outlines a forecast for the number of cities each with a population greater than 1 million. This study forecasts that China will have 128 cities meeting that criterion, more than the United States and Europe combined.[20]

In 1995, with the first wave of economic reform in full swing, 48 Chinese cities each had a population exceeding 1 million. By 2005, 28 more cities had joined the group, for a total of 76 cities meeting the threshold. By 2015, the United Nations forecasts, 112 Chinese cities will meet it, and by 2025, 163 cities. In that year, it is forecasted that 25 percent of the cities that each have more than 1 million people will be located in China. In the United States, Europe, and Japan, the number of cities will remain constant, with their share declining dramatically, as Figure 2.6 illustrates.

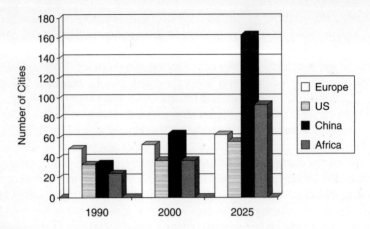

FIGURE 2.5 China Will Lead the Way in the World's Urbanization
Source: United Nations, 2012

The current economic and demographic trends are all challenging the formula that gave rise to China's economic miracle. Acting together, these trends create a cycle for change. Labor scarcity drives further wage increases. Manufacturing assets are moved, in many cases to lower-cost countries or, in some cases, moving inland to tap lower labor costs. Greater availability of economic opportunity inland leads to more widespread urbanization, lower migration, and greater labor scarcity. The aging of the working population and increased education accelerates the cycle (see Figure 2.7).

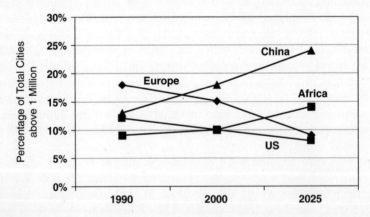

FIGURE 2.6 China Will Dominate in the Number of Cities with More Than 1 Million People Each
Source: United Nations, 2012

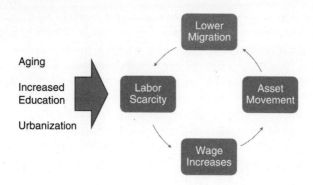

FIGURE 2.7 The Change Cycle in China's Economy

Although these economic and demographic trends are not new, the global economic recession of 2009 served as an accelerant. European demand fell dramatically and will in all likelihood remain low. China's trade surplus has begun to narrow. All of these trends are moving China away from its historical growth foundation. At the same time, these trends are moving the country toward a more balanced economy based on internal consumption. The source for the formula that will power the next phase of growth, both for China and the world, is the Chinese consumer.

The Rise of the Chinese Consumer

"In China, when you're one in a million, there are 1,300 people just like you." Bill Gates's memorable quote about China was spoken in the context of the large supply of well-educated, technically minded engineers available in China.[21] It also speaks to how trends, once they begin, gain momentum and scale at unprecedented rates.

China's population is more than 1.3 billion, which accounts for approximately one out of every five people on the planet. For a country this size, with the largest population in the world, the law of large numbers factors into every aspect of life, be it education, food, consumption, or income growth. Any trend, scaled with this population, becomes massive and often difficult to comprehend.

China does nothing small. Every societal trend seems to contain the words "the largest ever" or "unprecedented." Now those words are being applied to the growth of China's middle class. The middle class that is emerging in China today will become the largest in the world. Its size will power the next wave of not only China's economic growth but also the world's. It is happening so quickly that it seemingly defies reality, but real it is.

China today is a thriving consumer goods market. As China's export-growth model took hold and incomes rose, massive numbers of people started to enter the middle class. From 1995 to 2005, the population of China's middle class grew from close to zero to an estimated 87 million.[22] Today, China's middle class is already larger than the entire population of the United States and is expected to reach 800 million within the next 15 years.[23] Retail sales in the country have grown significantly, fueled by the rising incomes first brought about by the nation's export-led economic miracle.

China is already the largest market for many consumer categories. This includes automobiles: more than 13 million passenger cars were sold in 2010, and the demand is growing more than 30 percent annually. These sales have increased about tenfold in the past decade.[24] And even though China is already the largest market in the world, about 70 percent of the Chinese people have yet to buy a car, which highlights the dramatic economic growth potential remaining in the market.[25]

China is also the largest market for mobile phones, shoes, bicycles, motorbikes, and luxury goods. There are many categories for which China will soon become number one, including home appliances, Internet access, and jewelry.[26] The categories themselves illustrate the changing nature of China. The combination of owning a car, wearing jewelry, and carrying a mobile phone, as one billion Chinese do, provides a good portrait of the Chinese consumer, especially in the more prosperous coastal regions of the country.[27]

Even though China already commands a place among the largest of the world's consumer markets, the expansion pace continues to be high. Retail sales are growing about 18 percent a year.[28] Incomes, especially for the middle and upper classes, continue to rise. Credit Suisse reported that middle-class incomes increased 98 percent in 2004–2009, and upper-class incomes increased substantially more. Many believe that the amount of income available for discretionary spending is much higher than official government statistics suggest, because of a number of factors that include "gray" income: income that often goes unreported.

The forecasts for market size in just a few years' time are simply staggering. *Forbes* magazine cited the United Nations and Goldman Sachs in an article that stated, "Within a generation, the middle class in China will be roughly four times the size of the American middle-class population, according to the UN Population Division and Goldman Sachs. By 2030, China should have approximately 1.4 billion middle-class consumers compared to 365 million in the U.S. and 414 million in Western Europe."[29] Similarly, Procter & Gamble has presented data supporting its growth efforts in China that 270 million new middle-class consumers will be created in China in the next 10 years (see sidebar, "The Upside Seen by Established Players").[30]

Translating all of this into numbers yields a GDP that increases five times by 2025.[31] Chinese consumers are predicted to contribute approximately 25 percent of all consumption growth worldwide by that year. By the end of this decade, the consumer market will rise to a value close to $16 trillion. It is staggering and difficult to comprehend. And it is indeed happening faster than many believe.[32]

All of these millions of consumers coming into the middle class are not where you might think. They will live in cities that haven't been built yet but that will be built soon. They will live in cities with names that most people living outside China would not recognize. These cities will need subway systems, expressways, linkage to distribution through rail, and airports. All of this infrastructure is being created as both an instigator of and a response to the urbanization enveloping the country. These unprecedented changes are a transition from an agricultural-based society to a society led by an educated urban professional class. That transition also requires new support systems and social safety nets that spur the move toward increased consumption.

The Upside Seen by Established Players

Procter & Gamble (P&G) and Unilever are two firms that have a long-standing investment in China. Each company made strategic investments and entered the Chinese market near the beginning of economic reform. P&G entered China in 1988, and China has grown to be the company's second largest market in the world. Unilever entered the Chinese market in 1986. Each company was among the first of Western companies to enter the market. Despite their greater experience and longer time in penetrating the Chinese market, both companies see immense opportunity to capture in the next five years.

Unilever plans to increase the size of its China business by at least five times by 2019. To do so, the company's president in China is looking to capitalize on more affluent lifestyles by targeting food convenience. The company is also looking to leverage its relationships with Western retail chains as they expand into growing urban areas. Like P&G, Unilever is significantly increasing its production capacity within the country.

P&G believes that China is an integral part of its plan to reach 1 billion new consumers by the middle of this decade. Although China is now the company's second largest market, P&G estimates that around 400 million Chinese have yet to purchase any of its products. One of the pillars of P&G's growth strategy is to increase the number of categories

Continued

in which it competes. In the home market of the United States, P&G offers more than 35 categories of products to its consumers. In China, P&G goes to market with 15.

After P&G created the market for disposable diapers in the country, total P&G sales increased 10 times between 2000 and 2010. Its plans call on increasing that growth, citing a per capita usage that is less than 20 percent of its established, mature markets. Increasing the points of distribution is also part of the plan; P&G works directly with the central government on a project named 10,000 Villages, which is designed to create distribution networks in rural parts of the country. Starting in 2010, P&G's growth plan includes an additional $1 billion of investment in the market.

Notes

1. Cai Fang, "China's Rising Wages," East Asia Forum, September 5, 2011, www.eastasiaforum.org/2011/09/05/chinas-rising-wages.

2. Michelle Dammon Loyalka, "Chinese Labor, Cheap No More," *New York Times*, February 17, 2012, www.nytimes.com.

3. "Foxconn Raises Pay Rates Again at Chinese Factory," *Guardian*, October 1, 2010, www.guardian.co.uk/world/2010/oct/01/foxconn-raises-salaries-chinese-plant.

4. David Barboza, "Foxconn Plans to Lift Pay Sharply at Factories in China," *New York Times*, February 18, 2012, www.nytimes.com.

5. Chris Devonshire-Ellis, "China Now Has Third Highest Labor Costs in Emerging Asia," China Briefing, January 19, 2011, www.china-briefing.com/news/2011/01/19/china-near-top-of-the-list-for-wage-overheads-in-emerging-asia.html.

6. Jonathan Wright, Manisha Sahni, and Rowena Zamora, "Wage Increases in China: Should Multinationals Rethink Their Manufacturing and Sourcing Strategies?" *Accenture*, 2011, www.accenture.com/SiteCollectionDocuments/PDF/Accenture_Wage_Increases_in_China.pdf.

7. "The End of Cheap Chinese Labour?" *Economist*, July 18, 2010, www.economist.com/blogs/freeexchange/2010/07/china.

8. Sophie Leung, "Indonesia, Bangladesh 'Winners' as China Costs Rise, KPMG Says," Bloomberg, September 14, 2011, www.bloomberg.com/news/2011-09-15/indonesia-bangladesh-winners-as-china-costs-rise-kpmg-says.html.

9. Boston Consulting Group, "Made in the USA, Again: Manufacturing Is Expected to Return to America as China's Rising Labor Costs Erase Most Savings from Offshoring," press release, May 5, 2011. www.bcg.com/media/PressReleaseDetails.aspx?id=tcm:12-75973.

10. Chris Devonshire-Ellis, "China Now Has Third Highest Labor Costs in Emerging Asia," China Briefing, *China Briefing*, January 19, 2011, www.china-briefing. com/news/2011/01/19/china-near-top-of-the-list-for-wage-overheads-in-emerging-asia.html.

11. Yajun Zhang and Liyan Qi, "China Foreign Direct Investment Falls Again," *Wall Street Journal*, March 15, 2012, http://online.wsj.com/article/SB10001424052702 304459804577282430767244066.html.

12. China Exports, www.tradingeconomics.com/china/exports.

13. United Nations, "Data Bank," http://data.un.org.

14. "China's Achilles Heel," *Economist*, April 21, 2012.

15. Yao Li, John Whalley, Shunming Zhang, and Xiliang Zhao, "The Higher Educational Transformation of China and Its Global Implications," National Bureau of Economic Research, March 2008, www.nber.org/papers/w13849.

16. "Educated and Fearing the Future in China," *New York Times*, March 7, 2010, http://roomfordebate.blogs.nytimes.com/2010/03/07/educated-and-fearing-the-future-in-china.

17. CBI China Briefing, "Consumer Goods and Services in China," Slideshare, May 5, 2009, www.slideshare.net/thecbi/cbi-presentation-providing-goods-and-services-for-consumers-in-china-1451574.

18. Chris Oliver, "China's Urban Population Bigger Than Rural," *Market Watch*, January 17, 2012, www.marketwatch.com/story/chinas-urban-population-bigger-than-rural-2012-01-17.

19. George Stalk and David Michael, "What the West Doesn't Get about China," *Harvard Business Review*, June 2011, http://hbr.org/2011/06/what-the-west-doesnt-get-about-china/ar/2.

20. Rob Minto, "Chart of the Week: The 1M-Plus Cities," *Financial Times*, October 21, 2011, http://blogs.ft.com/beyond-brics/2011/10/21/chart-of-the-week-the-million-plus-cities/#axzz1qw7Wi7zn.

21. Bill Gates, *Impatient Optimist: Bill Gates in His Own Words*, ed. Lisa Rogak. Evanson, IL: Agate Publishing, 2012, p. 33.

22. "Understanding China's Middle Class," *China Business Review*, January 2009, www.chinabusinessreview.com.

23. Helen Wang, "Times Have Changed: No More 'China Produces and America Consumes,'" *Forbes*, February 6, 2011, www.forbes.com/sites/china/2011/02/06/times-have-changed-no-more-china-produces-and-america-consumes.

24. "China 2010 Auto Sales Reach 18 Million, Extend Lead," Bloomberg, January 10, 2011, www.bloomberg.com/news/2011-01-10/china-2010-auto-sales-reach-18-million-extend-lead-update1-.html.

25. Credit Suisse, "Credit Suisse Survey Shows Chinese Consumer Spending Jumps," press release, January 12, 2010, www.credit-suisse.com/news/en/media_release .jsp?ns=41389.

26. Stalk and Michael, "What the West Doesn't Get about China."

27. Russell Flannery, "China Mobile Phone Users Now Top One Billion," *Forbes*, March 30, 2012, www.forbes.com/sites/russellflannery/2012/03/30/china-mobile-phone-users-now-exceed-one-billion.

28. Chris Oliver, "China Consumers Spend, Even As Growth Eases," *Market Watch*, January 19, 2012, http://articles.marketwatch.com/2012-01-19/economy/ 30742555_1_consumer-inflation-china-consumers-credit-suisse.

29. Kenneth Rapoza, "Within a Generation, China's Middle Class Four Times Larger Than America's," *Forbes*, September 5, 2011, www.forbes.com/sites/kenrapoza/ 2011/09/05/within-a-generation-china-middle-class-four-times-larger-than-americas.

30. Presentation at the Procter & Gamble Analyst Meeting, December 16, 2010, Cincinnati, http://media.corporate-ir.net/media_files/irol/10/104574/HANDOUT-ANALYSTMEETING2010.pdf.

31. Jonathan Woetzel, Lenny Mendonca, Janamitra Devan, Stefano Negri, Yangmel Hu, Luke Jordan, Xiujun Li, Alexander Maasry, Geoff Tsen, and Flora Yu, "Preparing for China's Urban Billion," McKinsey Global Institute, February 2009.

32. Credit Suisse, "Credit Suisse Survey Shows Chinese Consumer Spending Jumps," press release.

CHAPTER 3

Catalysts for Consumption

China's economy continues its transition from an export-driven growth formula to an economy that is increasingly consumer-driven. As that transition has begun, many significant challenges are being addressed to eliminate barriers and increase its pace. China's export-driven model funneled business-focused investment capital into the SEZs targeted for growth.

To facilitate a smooth and quick transition, a broad-based infrastructure is necessary. This includes an interstate freeway system to enable market access. The infrastructure for the transition must include more than the physical, concrete type of assets like roads, railways, and airports. There must also be a social infrastructure to promote stability and greater discretionary spending. Today's state-run banking system is a barrier for entrepreneurs and small businesses seeking capital. The infrastructure for a consumer-driven economy also requires freer access to capital beyond what is currently in place.

These kinds of challenges are being addressed—all at once and rapidly—to promote the economic transition. Unlike mature economies that are constrained by debt and cautioned by austerity, China continues to act boldly in these areas. This boldness can be seen in the government's stimulus actions to uphold the economy during the global downturn of 2009. The Chinese government announced a $580 billion stimulus package in the fall of 2008.[1] With its large account surplus, China easily committed this level of spending without a severe effect on its deficit level. Many analysts believe the stimulus size to be understated, given the other government and bank-financed projects aimed at spurring growth. The stimulus moved into the economy quickly, spurring the saying *Jiakuai*, or "Build it quickly."

The government's bold actions can also be seen in its current five-year plan. Since the founding of the current government in 1949, the governing party has issued its plan for the economy every five years.

Although it was originally designed as the authoritative, top-down economic plan for the nation, more recent plans have been more like political documents outlining the government's political and investment priorities. The last plan, issued in early 2011, is focused on meeting the challenges with investments to help the country transition to a more consumer-centered economy. Private enterprise is also taking steps to promote infrastructure in other areas, making capital more freely available to entrepreneurs and providing financial services to consumers at higher rates of return. This is likely to spur higher levels of discretionary spending.

This chapter provides an overview of the key infrastructural components being addressed. It highlights the three investment components that act as catalysts to spur the country's economic transition (see Figure 3.1):

1. **Physical infrastructure.** This includes roads, bridges, railways, and other projects that facilitate the smooth flow of goods and people. China is making unprecedented, extraordinary strides in building a nationwide physical infrastructure.
2. **Financial infrastructure.** This involves the steps required to provide a foundation, incentives, and services that promote consumer confidence and discretionary spending. Because China has the highest household savings rates in the world, greater levels of certainty and more money management alternatives are needed.
3. **Capital infrastructure.** This enables increased sources and a smoother flow of investments to increase business formation and the breadth of nonmanufacturing business growth, which increases income, wealth, and discretionary spending.

The rest of this chapter provides more details on the current status and future plans of the infrastructure in these three areas.

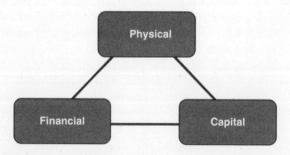

FIGURE 3.1 Key Infrastructure Areas Being Built

Build It Quickly: The Physical Infrastructure to Move Goods and People

In the five years from 2006 through 2010, about 7,200 kilometers (about 4,500 miles) of new expressway was built every year in China. It's an unprecedented amount. For comparison, the Chinese government built enough road every year, on average, for five straight years, that is greater than the distance from New York to San Francisco or from Madrid to Moscow. The building pace continues. Today, China's expressway system is second in the world only to that of the United States—an astonishing fact, given that few expressways even existed in China as recently as the 1980s. The Chinese government is also investing in building highways to complement the nationwide expressway system. From 2006 to 2012, China added 137,000 kilometers (about 85,000 miles) of new highway every year. That's an average of nearly 377 kilometers (about 235 miles) per day. Almost half of the country's installed base of road infrastructure was constructed in the last five years.

All of this is supported and enabled by an unprecedented level of government investment. Since the government stimulus that was announced in late 2008, investment in road construction increased more than 40 percent in 2009 and more than 20 percent in 2010. In those two years, the average annual government outlay for road construction was close to 1,200 billion yuan.[2] The costs have dwarfed those required to build the U.S. interstate highway system, which has often been referred to as the largest public works project in history.

It will probably still not be enough. Total freight traffic via roads is increasing at a faster rate than road construction in many areas. More than 14 million new cars came onto China's roads in 2011.[3] Congestion, occasionally at absurd levels, occurs frequently in the heavily urbanized eastern cities. In 2010 the *Economist* reported a traffic jam in Beijing that was more than 62 miles long and lasted for 11 days.[4]

To combat these challenges and connect the expressways that are separated, the government's current five-year plan, through 2015, seeks to finalize an expressway network of 10 major east-west and north-south arteries, referred to as the Five Verticals and Five Horizontals.[5] As of 2009, approximately 11 percent of the villages remained inaccessible by road, and the government intends to close much of this gap by 2015. Of the cities with a population greater than 200,000, 90 percent are expected to be connected to the expressway system. China's investment in road infrastructure is reaching the point at which a nationwide, connected expressway system will be in place.

Rail infrastructure was approximately 55 percent of the government's road investment during the few years leading up to 2010, with about 750 billion yuan spent in 2010 alone. Between 2006 and 2010, more than

8,000 miles of additional track was laid down. Yet the rail system remains very constrained. About 41 percent of China's railway system is double-tracked. On the 59 percent that is not, traffic bottlenecks often occur. In 2009 and 2010, an additional 100 million passengers were accommodated by the system. The total number of passengers on China's railways in 2010 was more than 1.6 billion.[6]

Despite its own congestion problems, China's road system has been able to absorb more capacity than its railways have. While freight traffic on roads is increasing 15 percent per year, freight traffic on rail is growing less than 10 percent. China's railway system is more constrained.

For both roads and railway, the primary culprit of the constraint is coal (see sidebar, "China and Coal"). China runs on coal. Most residential buildings are powered by it. The factory towns of the south are clouded in smog by it. All that coal being delivered via the roads and railways of China leaves little room for much else. One reason for the reportedly multiday gridlocks in Beijing is the hundreds of trucks overloaded with coal coming into the city from the coal-harvesting regions north of the city.

China and Coal

China has an insatiable appetite for coal. As much as 70 percent of China's energy is powered by it. China consumes more coal than any other country does, but its per capita consumption is very low, which means that coal consumption will continue to skyrocket.

Coal consumption has increased 200 percent in the last 10 years. In raw numbers, that's an average of 200 million tons per year in the past decade. The country's total consumption of coal in 2011 was 3.5 billion tons, and the pace of consumption continues to increase. Coal has always been the predominant fuel of choice for the country's manufacturing base. As wages have grown to produce a middle class, millions of cars and increased residential usage have driven a higher percentage of growth.

Compared to the coal usage of other countries, coal fills a much greater percentage of China's total energy needs. Most other countries have a broader mix of energy sources. Other emerging economies have different native sources. Brazil uses more oil. Russia uses more natural gas. China's native energy source is coal: the country holds more than 13 percent of the world's coal reserves. In developing its economy and its heritage of self-reliance, China used the energy it had and shaped its society to use it.

Continued

All that coal usage comes at a cost. The environmental pollution in China's major cities is extreme, and the infrastructure suffers from the high usage. All that coal has to be transported by railway, road, or water, taking up valuable capacity that could be reserved for goods or people. The railway capacity that is dedicated to bringing coal to the cities is staggering: 63 percent of freight traffic on the country's railways is for coal. That accounted for 2 billion tons of coal being transported by railway in 2010. The percentage rises to nearly 80 percent when coal-processing materials for smelting are included.

As the following graphic shows, not other material comes close to reaching the levels of coal transported by rail. Coal is not only the largest category, but the fastest growing category as well. China's rail system is almost exclusively dedicated to transporting coal, with little room left for anything else.

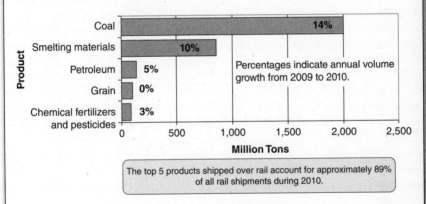

The top 5 products shipped over rail account for approximately 89% of all rail shipments during 2010.

The government's five-year plan calls for ambitious investments and targets in renewable energy. Hydroelectric power is the current major source for renewable energy, although it has been subject to both droughts and controversy in recent years. In spite of these efforts, the high growth rates for energy demand will most likely keep the trucks and railway cars full of coal for the foreseeable future.

Source: "Sustainable Growth in China: Spotlight on Energy," Goldman Sachs, August, 2012; Li & Fung, *China Distribution and Trading*, 93: 5 (December 2011)

The government is formulating policies to address these capacity constraints. Encouraging a more sustainable energy footprint is one strategy. The government's current five-year plan calls for the use of renewable energies and environmental taxes.[7] The plan also outlines the government's priority to continually invest in nuclear and hydroelectric energy to further offset coal dependency.[8] For example, China is in the midst of building its second west-to-east national gas pipeline, which will serve 400 million residents when complete and reduce coal dependency.[9]

For a thriving infrastructure that facilitates the movement of goods in a just-in-time environment, more people and coal have to use transportation alternatives to the existing railway and emerging road network. Twenty urban subway systems are being built in the largest urban centers as one alternative.

The greatest thrust to address the capacity constraint, however, and offer alternative transportation options is high-speed rail. High-speed rail is perhaps the government's most ambitious component of the infrastructure plan. The country now has nearly 4,000 miles of in-service high-speed rail, up from a mere 400 miles in 2008.[10] The planned network will connect the major cities of the east with the emerging inland urban centers, providing fast movement and access between the major commercial centers.

China already is approaching 40 percent of the world's high-speed rail capacity. This does not include the high-speed railways currently under construction or planned for construction. In that category, government plans call for putting more high-speed railways on the ground at more than twice the capacity of any other country in the world, as Figure 3.2 highlights. Almost one-third of high-speed rail construction will occur in China.

Traveling on high-speed trains will be expensive for the average Chinese citizen. As in many developing nations, the train has offered China almost a universal mode of transport. With millions of migrant workers traveling from rural inland regions to the export factories on the eastern coast, affordable railway travel has historically been a lifeline to the children and

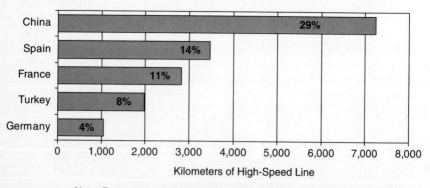

Note: Percentages indicate share of total global planned construction.

FIGURE 3.2 The Top 5 Countries with the Largest Footprint of High-Speed Rail
Source: International Union of Railways

other family members left· at home. One possibility of the change in passenger travel to the more expensive high-speed rail is that a government-imposed tax on the migrant workforce will encourage more people to stay home and seek prosperity there. In the interim, many workers are choosing to use the bus, and the demand for service in this industry is soaring.

At the project's end, China will have more than 8,000 miles of high-speed railway. This amount will give China more high-speed rail than anywhere else in the world (see Figure 3.3).

The planned network will come together in the·next few years as more and more lines become operational and interconnected. Passengers can now ride from Shanghai to Beijing in a few hours. The workforce in Tianjin, the first established SEZs and the home of companies like Motorola, can now arrive in Beijing within 30 minutes. High-speed rail from Shanghai, China's commercial center, is now linked with Chengdu, an inland province that is one of the gateways to the fastest growing geographical regions in the market.[11]

Until more passengers start using alternative modes of travel to the railway and less coal travels the network, it's likely that China's road and railway networks will be constrained. Road travel will provide the better

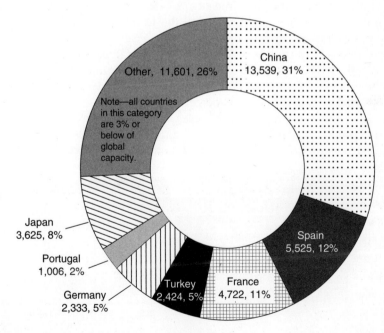

FIGURE 3.3 Share of Global High-Speed Rail, Post-Build

Source: International Union of Railways

option, with more ability to absorb additional capacity, but both systems will be stressed. As all of the massive investment in building China's road and railway network comes to fruition, it will provide the infrastructure to move goods more freely across the market.

Incentives to Increase Consumption

Once consumer goods arrive on the newly constructed roads, consumers will need to have the money to buy them and the confidence to spend it. Many Chinese consumers need help on both fronts, which are just as daunting as the lack of infrastructure was a few decades ago.

Chinese citizens are notoriously big savers. The savings rate in China is 31 percent of total income, higher by a significant margin than in other emerging economies. The savings rate in India is less than half of that in China, and the savings rate in Brazil is less than one-third (see Figure 3.4).[12] The differences are even more striking when China's rate is compared to the rates in the mature and developed markets of the United States and Western Europe.

Many have cited cultural reasons as the cause of the disproportionately high Chinese savings rate. Much of Chinese culture is rooted in Confucianism, which values thrift and frugality. Recent data suggest, however, that cultural considerations might not lie at the heart of the high savings rate. Survey data published by Credit Suisse suggests that China's household savings rate is bifurcated between the richer coastal regions and the emerging inland areas. In that survey, the largest cities in the country's eastern portion—Beijing, Shanghai, and Guangzhou—have witnessed household savings rates between 24 and 30 percent, lower than the country average.[13] Since consumers enjoy higher incomes in these cities, more discretionary spending is available to them, and correspondingly lower saving rates result. This is just one indication that the country's high savings rate can be

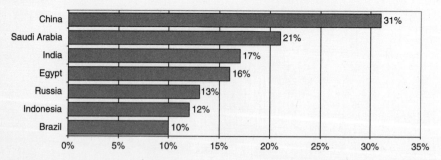

FIGURE 3.4 Savings as a Percentage of Household Income
Source: Data from Credit Suisse, 2011

explained more as a result of economically rational choices than Confucian values or other cultural roots.

China's high savings rate can also be explained by the extreme uncertainty that Chinese citizens have lived with throughout the country's history. As outlined in Chapter 1, the political campaigns conducted from the 1950s through the 1970s caused tremendous upheaval. For those who remember, a sense of self-preservation and caution most likely drives much of their actions in regard to savings. It is noteworthy that China's younger population, born after the era of political campaigns, shows a much higher propensity to consume and spend than their older counterparts do. For many Chinese, past is indeed prologue and a sign of continual caution.

In the 1990s, the Chinese government embarked on a significant reform of its state-owned enterprises, breaking the relationship with health care, pension, and housing, historically provided by these companies. What started out after the 1949 revolution as the vehicle for government control—the *dan wei* system described in Chapter 1—led later to the notion of the Iron Rice Bowl, in which state-owned companies became the chief provider of the country's social safety net. That system is now largely gone. In its place is a decentralized structure in which pensions are largely controlled at the municipal level, and its administration is highly varied across the country. This structure has led to greater uncertainty, and consumers have responded by saving more.

The current financial structure also encourages the high savings rate. For the vast majority of Chinese citizens, the bank and the mattress are the sole savings vehicles available. With interest rates controlled by the government and kept low, individuals struggle to maintain wealth at a pace that keeps up with inflation. Lacking market alternatives such as mutual fund investments, consumers recognize they need to save more money just to stay even.

This, however, is not the case for the more affluent Chinese on the coasts, where many have invested in the continuing appreciation of real estate to increase their wealth. But for the middle class in the more inland regions of the country, a lack of alternatives, a low rate of return, and uncertainty about health care and pension are keeping the savings rates high.

The current financial structure is in place to support the country's export-driven growth model. State-run banks offer only low interest returns to consumers, then use those funds to lend at significantly higher returns and profit disproportionately. The *New York Times* reported that government policies enacted a hidden tax on Chinese households that amounted to $36 billion in 2008, which amounts to a wealth transfer from Chinese households.[14]

The current financial structure may also be contributing to a widening income inequality. The Gini coefficient is the standard measure of income inequality, and China's rate of income inequality has been moving steadily upward to levels of concern.

All of these factors foster growing levels of uncertainty and, increasingly, protest actions by citizens.

Certainly, as expressed through the government's current five-year economic plan, these issues are recognized. The government has expressed the objective of improving the social safety net. For example, the government has outlined an objective to centralize pension administration from the municipal level up to the provincial level, creating more consistency and certainty. Broader access to consumer credit is progressing—though slowly, in the minds of many. Deregulation of the banking market, which would allow increased competition, consumer alternatives, and access to more wealth-producing options, has been slow.

One of the more notable government priorities has been the expressed goal of building more affordable housing. Escalating appreciation of real estate assets has been a recent concern in the economy. The appreciation of real estate has led to increasing wealth in the eastern provinces, which have been among the first areas of the country to deregulate and privatize the housing market. Local governments have employed the common practice of claiming ownership of land and offering compensation to the current residents far below market value, then profiting from the difference when the land is sold to developers. This is yet another example of government practice leading to a growing income gap.

Housing mortgages, though increasingly available, are not yet a mainstream option in China, and even so, high down-payment requirements also create a barrier to increased consumption. To help remove these barriers, the central government is increasing the bank levels of consumer lending and providing incentives for the consumer purchase of automobiles and housing appliances. China's current five-year plan calls for the construction of 36 million homes for low-income citizens by the year 2015.

The government recognizes the problem of citizens with ordinary levels of income and their anger at being priced out of real estate markets that have been driven higher by speculation.[15] Along with rising incomes, these steps will have an effect. Over time, as the banking markets progress through deregulation, more alternatives will become available to consumers and savings rates will probably decline, just as they have in the more prosperous coastal regions of the country.

The Free Flow of Capital

The Chinese city of Ordos was built in recent years to house nearly 1 million people. It was built in Inner Mongolia, the region north of Beijing, which has grown substantially in wealth because of its rich coal resources and the rest of the country's insatiable need for them. An eerie feeling awaits those who visit Ordos, because the city is largely vacant. There is hardly anyone there. *Time* magazine created a poster child for government waste when it published a photo essay of the city showing massive innumerable skyscrapers and pristine housing developments, all empty.[16] It is as though a neutron bomb had been dropped on the city, leaving no people but everything else intact.

There are other examples as well. Satellite imagery from Google Maps shows many instances of housing developments and corporate parks, all newly constructed, sitting empty.[17] As the government (really *governments*, since often the provincial governments act autonomously from the central government in Beijing) has sought to invest in infrastructure to address impending urbanization, capital has in some cases missed the mark. Economists often cite the state-run system, which dictates investment from a top-down government policy, as the reason for this. Banks essentially extend loans based on government directives and priorities rather than on assessments of risk and reward. As a result, capital is being misallocated. Moreover, many studies suggest that government-dictated investments are hampering the development of a nonmanufacturing service economy that would raise incomes and increase employment to fuel consumption.

Foreign direct investment and the growing presence of private equity are providing better access to capital, and this will resolve these problems and provide alternative sources of funding to fuel business growth, employment, and incomes. The *Economist*'s Intelligence Unit (EIU) issued a 2012 report on how foreign direct investment is changing in China. It noted two growing trends: the nonmanufacturing service sector and the proportion of foreign investment being funneled to China's inland regions. Within five years, the EIU predicted, nearly half of all foreign direct investment will migrate inland and away from the historical export centers of the coastal east. The study offered a fact-based comparison of foreign direct investment between 2001 and 2010. It showed a significant decrease in the amount of investment allocated to manufacturing and a subsequent increase in more service-intensive industries, as illustrated in Figure 3.5.

In 2001, fully 66 percent of all foreign direct investment was allocated to manufacturing. That level declined to 47 percent in 2010. Service-based industries like retail trade and commercial services have filled the gap. As usual, the eastern provinces are leading the way. Once home to a thriving and dominating export industry, the coastal city of Xiamen had 60 percent of its foreign direct investment allocated to service-based industries in 2009. This included areas such as retail trade and information technology (IT) services. As a result of tax incentives and the changing economic landscape putting a damper on exports, foreign investment is moving inland, with the eastern provinces capturing 60 percent of foreign investment, down from 80 percent in the mid-1990s.[18]

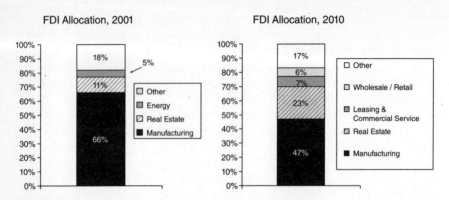

FIGURE 3.5 Comparison of Foreign Direct Investment Showing a Shift to Service-Based Industries

Private equity funds are also moving into the country as alternative capital sources for both established businesses and entrepreneurs. Through 2012, more than $22 billion in China-focused private equity was raised, down from 2011 but up from a standing start about five years ago. Increased appetite from institutional investors and limited access to investors through public markets will continue to stoke growth demand for private equity.[19] Early entry by established global funds is now giving rise to domestically created and managed private equity firms, with yuan-denominated funds now predominating. Private equity is in its infancy, and its percentage of investment relative to GDP is much lower than in other developing markets. As the presence of private equity grows, entrepreneurs and established businesses will have alternative options for capital, raising incomes and creating wealth that will drive the consumer-led economy forward.

China's infrastructure continues to make generational strides in the span of just a few years. Distribution points are rapidly expanding. With rising incomes, expanding credit, and a more deregulated financial sector on the horizon, the declines in the savings rates experienced in the eastern portions of the country will start to spread inland. Capital will become more widely available through more diversified foreign investment and a rising private equity industry that will spur an expanding service sector.

The past 30 years have seen China emerge onto the global economic stage from an era defined by destabilization and chaos. Low-cost labor, massive levels of migration, favorable government policies, and foreign investment have combined to create an economic powerhouse. China became the "factory of the world," exporting its labor-intensive, low–capital intensive manufacturing to create the toys, household goods, and other items bought by consumers in every other place in the world except China.

Now the world's eyes are turning to understand and tap into the next phase of global growth: China's domestic market. The effort to do so is increasingly viewed as a requirement for the economic vitality of the world's consumer-product companies. Many are already pushing ahead and succeeding. Others have tried, failed, and retreated. The difference lies in understanding the many dimensions of the market, the routes to market to reach these new consumers, and the capabilities required to utilize them. Those three things—market, channels, and capabilities—are the subjects of the next part of this book.

Notes

1. Calum MacLeod, "China's Economic Stimulus Plan Targets Its Infrastructure," *USA Today*, November 11, 2008, www.usatoday.com/money/world/2008-11-11-China_N.htm.

2. Li & Fung Research Centre, "An Update on the Transport Infrastructure Development in China: Road Transportation (2011)," August 2011, www.funggroup.com/eng/knowledge/research/china_dis_issue87.pdf.

3. Bertel Schmitt, "2011 New Car Sales around the World: China Crawls," Truth about Cars, January 12, 2012, www.thetruthaboutcars.com/2012/01/2011-new-car-sales-around-the-world-china-crawls.

4. "The Great Crawl of China," *Economist*, August 26, 2010, www.economist.com/node/16909167.

5. Andrew Galbraith, "All about the Fives: China's Transportation Plans," *Wall Street Journal*, March 22, 2012, http://blogs.wsj.com/chinarealtime/2012/03/22/all-about-the-fives-chinas-transportation-plans.

6. Li & Fung, "An Update on the Transport Infrastructure Development in China."

7. Jonathan Watts, "China Plots Course for Green Growth amid a Boom Built on Dirty Industry," *Guardian*, February 4, 2011, www.guardian.co.uk/world/2011/feb/04/china-green-growth-boom-industry.

8. "Wen Outlines Aggressive Green Initiative in Draft 5-Year Plan," Clean Biz Asia, March 7, 2011, www.cleanbiz.asia/story/wen-outlines-aggressive-green-initiative-draft-5-year-plan.

9. Daniel Bardsley, "Full Steam Ahead for China's Infrastructure Plans," *National*, September 28, 2011, www.thenational.ae/thenationalconversation/industry-insights/economics/full-steam-ahead-for-chinas-infrastructure-plans.

10. "Off the Rails?", *Economist*, March 31, 2011.

11. David Michael, "The Year of the Metal Rabbit: China's High-Speed Rail Network," *Business Week*, February 9, 2011, www.businessweek.com/globalbiz/content/feb2011/gb2011027_953097.htm.

12. Credit Suisse, "China Consumer Survey 2011," January 17, 2011.

13. Ibid.

14. David Barboza, "As Its Economy Sprints Ahead, China's People Are Left Behind," *New York Times*, October 9, 2011, www.nytimes.com.

15. Alan Wheatley, "Analysis: Why the World Should Heed China's Five-Year Plan," Reuters, March 7, 2012, www.reuters.com/article/2011/03/07/us-china-economy-plan-idUSTRE7261J820110307.

16. Michael Christopher Brown (photographer), Ordos, "China: A Modern Ghost Town," *Time*, www.time.com/time/photogallery/0,29307,1975397,00.html.

17. "China's Ghost Towns: New Satellite Pictures Show Massive Skyscraper Cities Which Are *Still* Completely Empty," *Daily Mail*, June 18, 2011, www.dailymail .co.uk/news/article-2005231/Chinas-ghost-towns-New-satellite-pictures-massive-skyscraper-cities-STILL-completely-empty.html.

18. "Serve the People: The New Landscape of Foreign Investment into China," *Economist Intelligence Unit*, 2012. www.eiu.com/public/topical_report .aspx?campaignid=chinafdi2012.

19. "China Sees Continued Private Equity (PE) Activity Amid a Year of Historic Change," www.ey.com/Publication/vwLUAssets/PE_in_China_unprecedented_growth_2012_ recap/$FILE/China_sees_continued_private_equity_activity_amid_a_year_of_ historic_change.pdf.

PART II

Markets, Channels, and Capabilities

CHAPTER 4

One Country, Many Markets

The scale of China is both unique and awesome. With nearly 6 million square miles, China is the fourth largest country in the world by land mass. With an estimated population of 1.3 billion, China has the most people of any country in the world. Only India comes close, with 1.2 billion people. After that, you have to subtract a full 1 billion people to arrive at the third most populous country in the world: the United States, with a population of a mere 313 million.[1] To fully tap China's vast consumer market, one must cover a lot of land.

To complicate matters, there is a broad diversity to consider in any plan to reach all of the consumers in this large area. The southern part of the country is tropical; it feels like a sauna a good portion of the year. The northern part of the country experiences bitter, freezing winters. Although Mandarin is the official language of both commerce and government, multiple dialects are spoken and can be incomprehensible to one another. There are vast mountain ranges and deserts. Household incomes span a wide spectrum, from destitution to great wealth.

If you add the dizzying pace of development to the country's large scale, diversity and business planning can soon become an overwhelming process filled with uncertainty. Where does one start? If a company has an already established presence in the market, how does it recalibrate? Where are the central points of consumer demand that will drive the next phase of growth? How should efforts be prioritized?

There is a lot to work through. The size of the market opportunity and the complexity of the country suggests that resource prioritization will be critical to any company's future success. If the one-size-fits-all approach was ever valid, it certainly is no longer sufficient here. Different approaches will be required in different parts of the market. Because of China's diversity—economic, demographic, and geographic—companies need a way to break down the Chinese market into components that take these diverse factors into account, but also at a level that is pragmatic. Detailed frameworks will be hard to work with, so a framework at a manageable level is key.

To find the right level, China's governing administrative levels were used as the basis in analyzing data. Analogous to the state level in the governing of the United States, this level of government in China includes 22 provinces, 5 autonomous regions, and 4 municipalities.[2] These 3 areas comprise 31 geographical areas in total. Analyzing data at this level provides a manageable data set that produces insight about the various market conditions inside China.[3] A list of the names in each of these three areas is contained in Table 4.1. For purposes of simplicity, all of these areas will be referred to as provinces in this chapter, although they also include the larger municipal areas of Beijing, Shanghai, Tianjin, and Chongqing.

As outlined in Chapter 5, a province-level market analysis is also consistent with a channel view of the market. For instance, many of the legacy state-run retailers tend to focus regionally, with various levels of market presence province to province. Understanding total market potential at a province level aligns with competitive strategy activities. The role of government relations and oversight also tends to vary widely from province to province, so an analysis at this level is helpful there as well.

Macroeconomic data from 31 China provinces was collected and analyzed, providing a starting point to answer these questions and comprehend how the Chinese consumer market breaks down into different segments. The data sets are as follows:

- **Disposable income per person.** Companies need to prioritize their efforts in areas where people have high discretionary incomes and the resources to consume the products.
- **Annual growth rate of disposable incomes for urban residents.** China's National Bureau of Statistics reports that the vast majority—nearly 87 percent—of all retail sales occurs in cities. Growth rates in urban disposable incomes can help companies to anticipate and pinpoint the locations of rapidly emerging consumer demand.

TABLE 4.1 List of China's Administrative Areas

Provinces	Autonomous Regions	Municipalities
Anhui, Fujian, Gansu, Guangdong, Guizhou, Hainan, Hebei, Heilongjiang, Henan, Hubei, Hunan, Jiangsu, Jiangxi, Jilin, Liaoning, Qinghai, Shaanxi, Shandong, Shanxi, Sichuan, Yunnan, Zhejiang	Guangxi, Inner Mongolia, Ningxia, Tibet, Xinjiang	Beijing, Chongqing, Shanghai, Tianjin

- **Total population.** Total population lends insight into the number of potentially available consumers at the province level, a detail that is manageable to comprehend.
- **Land area.** The land area of each province, combined with its population, provides insight into the concentration level of consumer markets. Density is used as a proxy for degree of urbanization and provides insight on the accessibility of consumer markets and an investment's "bang for the buck" in each provincial market.

Each of these data sets provides a focus on individual criteria that are important in segmenting the Chinese market. Disposable income per person and the annual growth rate of urban disposable income provide insight into the consumer's capacity and propensity to buy. Companies need to target areas of the country where consumers have higher discretionary incomes. Total population numbers provide insight into the size of local markets. There is no need to focus on a particular local market with high discretionary incomes if there are only a few of these consumers. Land area is then matched with total population to determine population density; this measure targets accessibility. Combining the four data sets yields a segmentation model that highlights areas with large, dense populations with high discretionary incomes. Figure 4.1 shows these linkages.

The analysis starts with an examination of disposable income levels and growth rates, as outlined in Figure 4.2.

Findings from each of these key elements of the data shine a light on how to tap into China's prospective consumers. Provincial data using each of these metrics is examined in the sections below. After the results of each data set are examined separately, the data sets are consolidated and used to develop a geographical segmentation model for the Chinese market.

Data Input by Province	Segmentation Criteria
Disposable Income per Person Annual Growth Rate of Disposable Income for Urban Residents Total Population Land Area	(1) Capacity / Propensity to Buy 　• Levels of Discretionary Income 　• Growth Rates (2) Market Size (3) Market Accessibility 　• Population Density

FIGURE 4.1 Segmentation Model Design

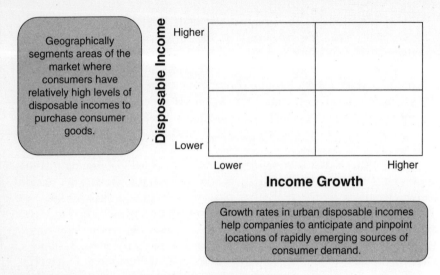

FIGURE 4.2 Analysis of Disposable Income of Chinese Consumers

Disposable Income: Who's Got the Most?

The great strides in wealth created in the SEZs have resulted in consumers with the highest disposable incomes residing in these areas. Shanghai, Beijing, and Tianjin are examples of cities where China's consumer market is thriving. These three cities constitute the center of the booming market for luxury goods. Guangdong, whose chief city is Shenzhen (highlighted in Chapter 1), is one of several provinces today whose residents enjoy the highest disposable incomes in the country.

Sitting in the middle tier of the disposable income spectrum are provinces that, in most cases, lie further inland. As outlined in the next section on income growth, these provinces are the up-and-comers, poised to rise and sit alongside the provinces that benefited most from China's export generation.

The bottom tier for disposable income consists of the provinces that border China's western end. These include Xinjiang, China's westernmost province, Tibet, and Qinghai. The province of Sichuan, recovering from the tragic and devastating earthquake in 2008, also lies in the bottom tier.

Urban Income Growth Rates: Emerging Consumers

In what parts of China are urban incomes growing the fastest? It may not be where you think. This is because incomes are growing the fastest in provinces with names that are not as familiar as the cities of Beijing and

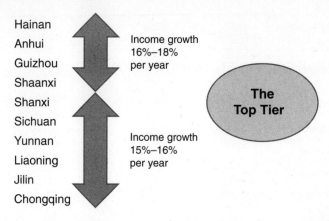

Hainan
Anhui
Guizhou
Shaanxi
Shanxi
Sichuan
Yunnan
Liaoning
Jilin
Chongqing

Income growth
16%–18%
per year

Income growth
15%–16%
per year

The
Top Tier

FIGURE 4.3 Top 10 Provinces in Urban Income Growth, 2010–2011 (from Highest Growth to Lowest Growth)

Shanghai. Figure 4.3 lists the 10 fastest growing provinces in urban income growth from 2010 to 2011.

A few of these provinces may be recognizable to those who have been working in or analyzing China's consumer market. Yet it is interesting to note that the areas most often in the international media's spotlight are absent. All but three of the top-tier provinces lie inland. The provinces that do lie on the coasts—Hainan, Jilin, and Liaoning—did not fully participate in the last generation's growth story. They are located outside the epicenter of already established regions.

What about the more widely known, established areas? How did they stack up? At least in terms of income expansion, the answer is in the bottom half. Figure 4.4 lists the bottom 10 provinces by income growth.

There they are: Beijing, Tianjin, and Guangdong are at the bottom of the income-growth pack. Shanghai province ranked nineteenth among the 31 provinces in our analysis. Granted, growth rates in this tier in every developed market in the world would be the envy of the marketer of consumer goods. Yet these figures speak to the larger story happening in the provinces that benefited from the export miracle: income growth is beginning to plateau in these local markets, which are increasingly mature and competitive.

The other significant finding from the analysis of the bottom pack of income growth rates is the presence of the outlying areas in the far west of the country. Tibet and Qinghai are provinces in this category. Xinjiang, the province that is farthest west in China, just missed making the bottom ten, ranking number 20 of the 31 provinces studied. Again, while the growth rates are high relative to the moderate pace of today's mature economies,

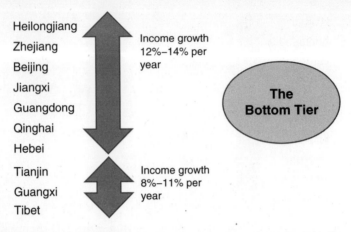

FIGURE 4.4 Bottom 10 Provinces in Urban Income Growth, 2010–2011 (from Highest Growth to Lowest Growth)

they do not occur where the fastest rising pools of China's consumers are emerging. With some exceptions to prove the rule, those pools are happening in China's central provinces.

Figure 4.5 highlights the location of each of the top 10 provinces to provide an understanding that income growth is occurring fastest outside the most widely known parts of the country.

Getting a Fuller Picture

The two macroeconomic data sets examined so far, disposable income levels and corresponding urban income growth rates, start to paint a picture of how the consumer economy is evolving. The highest disposable income levels reside in the export centers of the coastal east. However, the growth rates in income are happening further inland, toward the geographical center.

Adding population and population density to the analysis creates a fuller picture of where the current and emerging pools of consumer demand reside. High incomes and high income growth rates are less meaningful if they occur in provinces with fewer people. Furthermore, if a specific geographical area has a dispersed population, access to those potential consumers becomes more complex, requiring more investment. This analysis targets high population centers with dense urban environments populated by consumers with high and rising disposable incomes. That, of course, is the ideal.

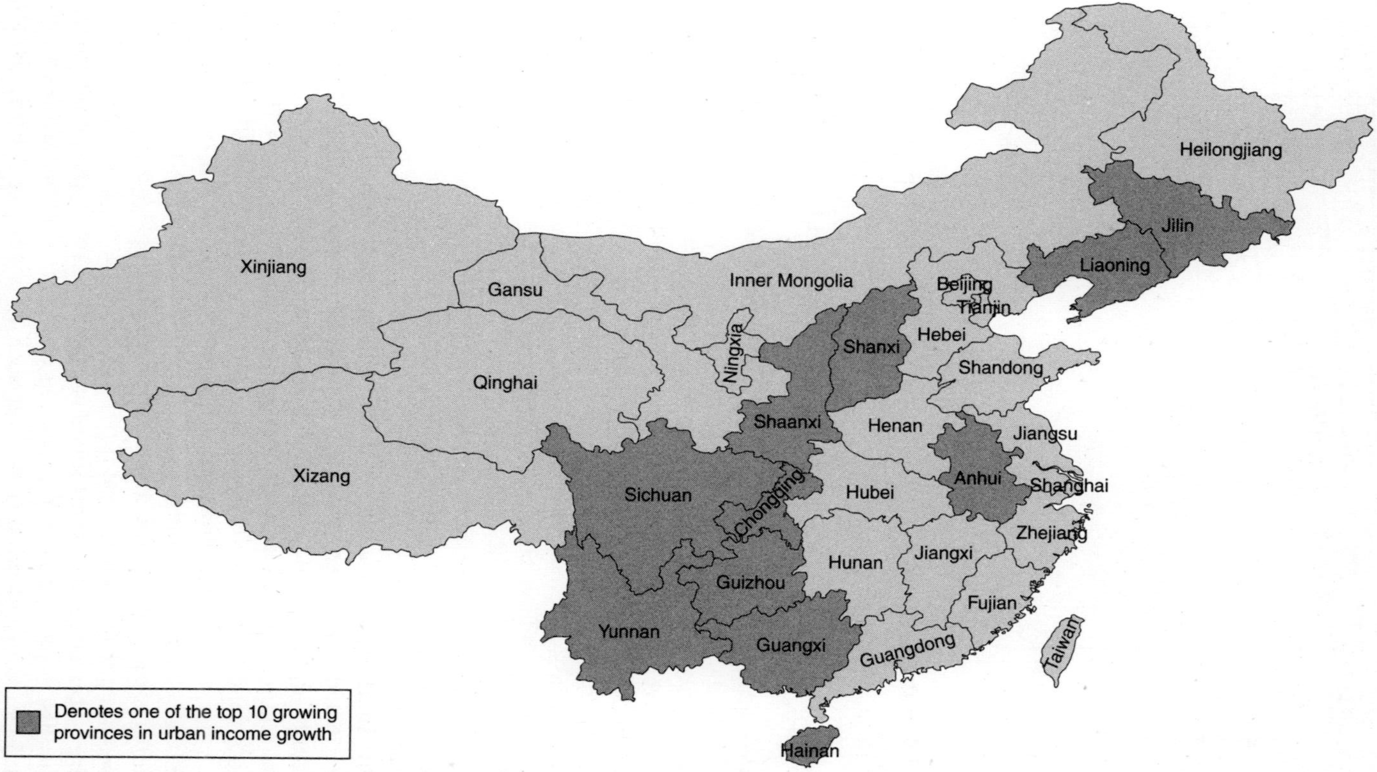
Heilongjiang
Jilin
Liaoning
Xinjiang
Gansu
Inner Mongolia
Beijing
Tianjin
Hebei
Ningxia
Shanxi
Shandong
Qinghai
Shaanxi
Henan
Jiangsu
Xizang
Sichuan
Chongqing
Hubei
Anhui
Shanghai
Zhejiang
Hunan
Jiangxi
Guizhou
Fujian
Yunnan
Guangxi
Guangdong
Taiwan
Hainan
Denotes one of the top 10 growing provinces in urban income growth

FIGURE 4.5 The 10 Provinces with the Highest Income Growth

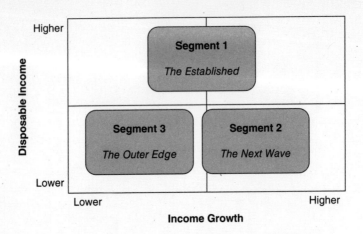

FIGURE 4.6 Three Geographical Segments of China's Consumer Market

Common areas of provinces start to emerge and are illustrated in Figure 4.6.

Three geographical segments may be identified, as follows:

1. **The established.** The first segment comprises the provinces with more developed, mature economies. These include Shanghai, Beijing, Tianjin, Guangdong, Jiangsu, and Fujian. All of these provinces are located in the eastern third of the country, have the highest available discretionary incomes, and are top tier in population density. If your company is selling consumer goods in China, its products are likely selling here, where the company's point of entry is located. While these provinces have an imposing force and sizable populations, their total population accounts for only approximately 25 percent of China's entire population.

2. **The next wave.** The second segment comprises the provinces that are leading the next emerging wave of Chinese consumers. They include Anhui, Hainan, Guizhou, Shaanxi, Shanxi, Yunnan, Sichuan, and Chongqing. Urban residents in these provinces are experiencing significantly higher growth rates in income. Furthermore, the population density of most of these provinces is in the upper two tiers and will only increase as urbanization continues. The province of Anhui shows particular promise as a candidate to lead this group of emerging consumer-growth provinces.

3. **The outer edge.** The third segment comprises two types of provinces. The first type consists of provinces adjacent to either economically established or emerging provinces, such as Shandong, Hubei, Hunan,

and Jilin. As economic growth expands from the established and emerging centers, these adjacent provinces benefit; they will be referred to as *fast followers*.

The second type consists of provinces located in the far west of the country, such as Tibet, Xinjiang, Gansu, and Qinghai. These provinces have not yet shown any indication of emerging pools of consumers. Low incomes, relative geographical isolation, and small dispersed populations will continue to be barriers toward these provinces embracing China's consumer revolution. Although the central government continues to funnel significant development projects and infrastructure to these regions, these provinces have been the source of much controversy and civic unrest in the past few years. These provinces are also the main sources of China's ethnic diversity, and interethnic conflicts have no doubt acted as another barrier toward economic progress, adding risk and therefore warranting caution on the part of companies looking to reach potential consumers in these areas.

Figure 4.7 shows the detail of the analysis at the provincial level and how these data sets come together.

The following data points are used:

- The *x*-axis plots each province's annual rise in urban incomes between the most current available years, 2010 and 2011.
- The *y*-axis plots each province's current level of disposable income per person.
- For each province, the size of each circle represents the relative size in population compared to the other provinces. For instance, in the top half of the chart, you can see that Guangdong has a much larger circle, and therefore a much larger population base, than Shanghai.
- The shading of each circle denotes the population density, measured in number of people per square kilometer. For example, Beijing is located near the top of the chart and is denoted in black. That indicates high density and a large number of consumers in a relatively small area. Qinghai, near the bottom of the chart center-left, is an example of a province at the other end of the density spectrum. The white color of the circle indicates a widely dispersed population. The small size of Qinghai's circle indicates a much smaller population relative to other provinces.

This analysis highlights a starting point for how to geographically segment China's many markets. It shows areas of established consumer markets as well as the emerging areas that form the next wave of consumer demand.

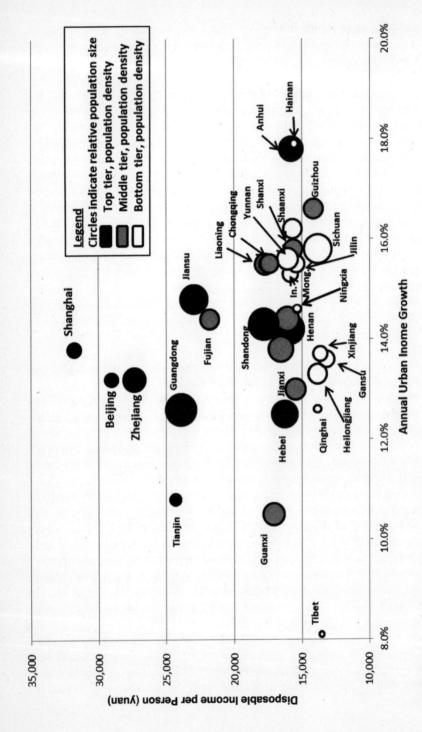

FIGURE 4.7 Finding the Current and Emerging Areas of Consumer Growth

Consumer Demand Clusters

How do these insights translate to a plan to reach more consumers? What do they mean in terms of prioritizing scarce resources? How can these insights be used to build a plan to further penetrate the market? The existing geographical breakdown of the country's different regions is not designed to specifically answer these questions.

Many companies use the same geographical segmentation as the central government. There are a few benefits to this approach. One basic benefit is that the government, through the National Bureau of Statistics, releases data according to its defined categories. Incorporating and analyzing data from this key data source is easier simply because it is the most commonly used segmentation of the market. For instance, when a leading bank states that growth in the southwest region was higher than planned, people familiar with this segmentation will be aware that the provinces of Chongqing and Chengdu are included in this region, according to the central government's definition.

But there are disadvantages to using this model as well. The segmentation provided by the National Bureau of Statistics is not specifically designed to organize a penetration and distribution strategy. It does not facilitate an understanding of how to organize most effectively around the current and future centers of consumer demand. For that, a new approach to segmentation is required.

To answer these questions, the analysis of provincial economic data was used to group the 31 Chinese provinces into key areas. Instead of targeting hundreds of cities across 31 provinces, companies and individuals developing plans to serve the market and reach more consumers can organize their efforts around four key areas of the country. Each of these four key areas, called a *demand cluster*, is a geographical location comprising a group of adjacent provinces. These demand clusters are defined by the following criteria and characteristics:

- The name of each cluster denotes the center of the cluster, which is a focal point of consumer demand. The centers of all the clusters are likely to become the centers of all commercial activity in China's consumer marketplace. They are hot zones for already established or emerging consumer demand, with close proximity to the largest and fastest growing markets in the country.
- Provinces that are fast followers (as described earlier) are grouped on the circumference of each cluster. These areas are less of an initial focus as compared to other provinces. China's growing infrastructure will provide accessibility to these markets as their growth prospects increase.

Data Input, by Province	Segmentation Criteria	Demand Cluster Design
Disposable Income per Person	(1) Capacity / Propensity to Buy • Levels of Discretionary Income • Growth Rates	Demand Hot Zones in the Center of Each Demand Cluster
Annual Growth Rate of Disposable Income for Urban Residents	(2) Market Size	Fast Follower Provinces Grouped around Outer Ring of the Demand Cluster
Total Population	(3) Market Accessibility • Population Density	Areas of Least Potential Lie Farthest from the Center
Land Area		Strive for Geographical/ Population Balance

FIGURE 4.8 Demand Cluster Design

- The areas with the least potential, either because of low population density or slower-growing incomes, lie farthest from the center of each cluster.
- Each demand cluster is a geographical area with a commonality in its consumer preferences and is proportional to the population and geography of the country at large.

These factors are illustrated in Figure 4.8.

The four demand clusters emanating from this approach are named as follows:

1. Guangdong
2. Beijing
3. Anhui
4. Chengdu

Table 4.2 and Figure 4.9 list each of the provinces and show the geographic location of each demand cluster, followed by a summary of each cluster's composition.

The Guangdong Demand Cluster

The Guangdong cluster comprises seven provinces lying at the heart of China's export machine. Guangdong has the highest population of any of the economically established provinces—large, urban, dense populations with high discretionary incomes. The cluster represents the core of China's luxury market, which is rapidly becoming the largest in the world. Five of these provinces—Jiangxi, Hunan, Hainan, Guangxi, and Fujian—are

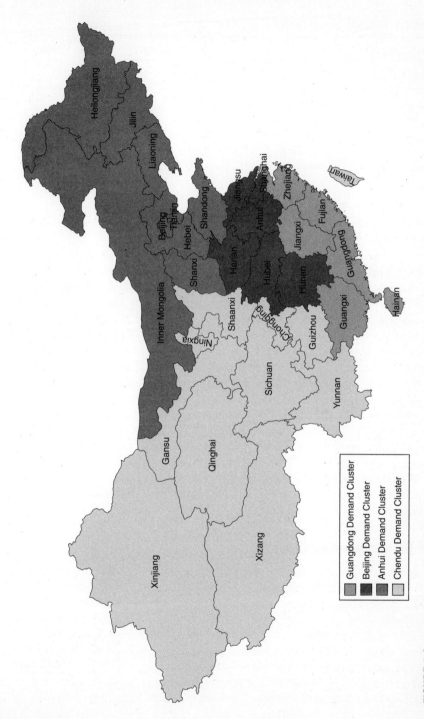

FIGURE 4.9 Map of Demand Clusters

TABLE 4.2 Province List of Demand Clusters*

Guangdong Cluster	Beijing Cluster	Anhui Cluster	Chengdu Cluster
Guangdong	Beijing	Anhui	Sichuan
Fujian	Heilongjiang	Henan	Chongqing
Guangxi	Hebei	Hubei	Gansu
Hainan	Inner Mongolia	Hunan	Guizhou
Jiangxi	Jilin	Jiangsu	Ningxia
Shanghai	Liaoning		Qinghai
Zhejiang	Shandong		Shaanxi
	Shanxi		Xinjiang
	Tianjin		Tibet
			Yunnan

* Provinces listed in alphabetical order.

adjacent to Guangdong. With the exception of Hainan, which has leading income growth rates, these provinces are fast followers: they have yet to develop current high incomes or high income growth rates, but they are expected to grow as Guangdong's consumption footprint expands.

Up the coast, the demand cluster extends through Fujian and Zhejiang to Shanghai. In terms of proximity, Shanghai lies closer to the Anhui demand cluster. The reasons for its inclusion here are the established infrastructure on the coast between Shanghai and Guangdong, the established manufacturing base between the two areas that could be retooled for domestic consumption, and the more common consumer characteristics that exist and are likely to develop. Zhejiang has an established economy that offers a base of potential consumers with the highest discretionary incomes in very densely populated areas.

The Guangdong demand cluster includes 20 percent of China's total population, has the highest disposable incomes on average, and has a total spending power of 6,016 billion yuan (about $955 billion).

The Beijing Demand Cluster

Up north from Guangdong lies the Beijing demand cluster, a collection of nine provinces with the highest disposable incomes in the country. In this cluster, wealth and the current consumer market are concentrated in Beijing and Tianjin.

Four of the remaining seven provinces in this cluster are followers, with current income levels and growth rates at a level below the top-priority markets today. These are the provinces that form a ring around Beijing: Hebei, Shanxi, Shandong, and Liaoning. Shandong is probably the leading emerging candidate in this group, given its relatively larger population.

Farther out of the center lie provinces that have yet to reach the economic level and promise of top- and middle-tier provinces. These are Heilongjiang, Jilin, and Inner Mongolia, which sit on the northern border of the country. Heilongjiang is an example of an outer-ring province.

The Beijing demand cluster offers high disposable incomes, access to 27 percent of China's total population, and a total spending power of 6,244 billion yuan (about $991 billion). The majority of that spending power, as noted earlier, lies in the densely populated areas of Beijing and Tianjin.

The Anhui Demand Cluster

Located about 300 miles inland, the city of Hefei is the capital of the Anhui province and one of the two focal points for the next wave of China's consumer demand. Anhui and its capital city are not widely covered by the international media. For the span of China's history, Hefei has often taken a backseat to the other cities as distribution points. From Shanghai, the historical trading routes to China's inland markets went up the Yangtze River through Chongqing. As high-speed rail and other infrastructure have been built in recent years, the logistical barriers between landlocked Anhui and other parts of the country have fallen. A trip from Shanghai to Anhui would have taken 15 hours a few decades ago and been fraught with uncertainty. Today it's a few hours, either up the expressway or by high-speed train.

Anhui's consumer economics are unique and promising; the province may be one of the largest emerging pools of future consumer demand. Anhui provides many characteristics that illustrate its future promise:

- It leads the country in the growth rates of urban discretionary spending.
- It is among the top-tier provinces in population density, comprising many densely populated urban centers.
- In terms of raw population, it ranks eighth among the 31, and it is one of the most populated provinces outside the established coastal economies.
- In terms of demographics, it is historically an agriculturally based, relatively poor area, but now rapid urbanization and industry investment portend a more rapid rise than in other provinces.

Four other provinces—Henan, Hubei, Hunan, and Jiangsu—make up the Anhui demand cluster and lie on Anhui's western edge. With neighboring access, both Hubei and Jiangsu offer high potential growth because of their dense populations, high disposable incomes (especially in Jiangsu), sizable populations, and solid income growth rates.

The Anhui demand cluster offers a focus on the next wave of consumer demand, access to 27 percent of China's total population, and a total spending power of 6,171 billion yuan (about $979 billion). As a group, this cluster offers the highest growth rates in urban income and contains the greatest population density. It is the leading focal point for the next wave of China's vast emerging consumer class. The city of Hefei is the key to the next wave of consumer growth in China and is the subject of Chapter 8.

Anhui's growing economic success can be attributed to its growing economic integration eastward. This demand cluster is designed to tap the next focal point in consumer demand at the cluster's center, then expand westward into the adjacent provinces, providing greater leverage in the efforts toward broader consumer reach.

The Chengdu Demand Cluster

Farther to the west lies a second focal point for the next wave of consumer demand. Chengdu, the capital city of the Sichuan province, and Chongqing, the capital city of the small province by the same name, form the center of this demand cluster. Metropolitan Chongqing is one of the largest urban areas in China. With a population approaching 29 million, metropolitan Chongqing will be one of the megacities that defines China's wave of urbanization.

The *Economist*'s Intelligence Unit forecasts that the city of Chongqing will be the fourth largest destination of foreign capital, rising above the cities of Beijing and Shanghai. Large manufacturers like Foxconn and Intel have established a foothold and a growing presence in the province. This rise in investment is, in part, driving a dramatic shift in migration and urbanization within Chongqing, in contrast to its history as a source of migrant labor for the coastal provinces. The rise in investment will also stoke the furnace of future consumer demand.[4]

Sichuan is Chongqing's neighboring province. Geographically speaking, Sichuan dwarfs Chongqing's size and is one of the largest populated provinces. Historically poor and rural, Sichuan was the primary source of migrant labor in the southeast provinces to fuel China's export machine. Those migration patterns are now reversing. In the period of five years starting in 2007, Sichuan has experienced a large influx of foreign capital.

Bordering the provinces at the center are other members of this group that are fast followers: Yunnan, Shaanxi, and Ningxia. Farther west lie the relatively economically dormant provinces: Qinghai, Gansu, Tibet, and Xinjiang. The developing infrastructure will rapidly provide access to these markets when the timing of their rise becomes more apparent and when the more economically attractive provinces near the core of the cluster are actively penetrated.

The Chengdu demand cluster offers a focus on the next wave of consumer demand, access to 26 percent of China's total population, and a total spending power of 5,165 billion yuan (about $820 billion). The Chengdu cluster contains the lowest disposable incomes per person and the lowest aggregate spending power of the four defined demand clusters. It also comprises, by a wide margin, the greatest geographical breadth. This analysis suggests that initial efforts in penetration and distribution be allocated to the focal point in the Chengdu-Chongqing area.

The Clusters as Focal Points for Consumer Demand

Together, these four defined demand clusters represent the central points of today established and growing consumer economy. Perhaps more important, they also help to organize go-to-market and distribution strategies in the emerging focal points of the next wave. The demand clusters are designed and grouped to facilitate business planning and provide balance market coverage.

Table 4.3 summarizes the consumer economic indicators for each of the four defined demand clusters. Focused on the central points of demand, the clusters provide a balanced coverage of population, income growth rates, and geographical reach.

The Beijing and Guangdong demand clusters form central zones for today's established and vibrant consumer economy. Fast approaching, and therefore more relevant, are the focal points of future demand, the Anhui and Chengdu demand clusters. The construction and definition of these four zones form a framework to help organize, prioritize, and plan a go-to-market and distribution plan to maximize value in China's consumer economy.

TABLE 4.3 Summary of Consumer Economics by Demand Cluster

Demand Cluster	Percentage of Total China Population	Average Disposable Income per Person (yuan)	Average Growth in Urban Income	No. of Provinces	Average Population Density (per sq km)	Total Spending Power (yuan) (USD)
Guangdong	20%	22,656	14.2%	6	425	6,016 billion (approximately $955 billion)
Beijing	27%	18,435	14.0%	9	144	6,244 billion (approximately $991 billion)
Anhui	27%	17,457	15.0%	5	435	6,171 billion (approximately $979 billion)
Chengdu	26%	14,902	13.9%	11	60	5,165 billion (approximately $820 billion)

Notes

1. CIA Fact Book, China, https://www.cia.gov/library/publications/the-world-fact-book/geos/ch.html.

2. Ibid.

3. Author's note: Taiwan, considered a province by the People's Republic of China, is excluded from this analysis. Hong Kong and Macau are also excluded from this analysis.

4. "Serve the People: The New Landscape of Foreign Investment into China," *Economist Intelligence Unit*, 2012, www.eiu.com/public/topical_report.aspx?campaignid=chinafdi2012.

CHAPTER 5

Channels to a Growing Market

As companies strive to reach China's vast market, a gold rush dynamic has taken hold. The orderly progression of sequential, proven investment return is not the ruling order of the day. Instead, the primary driver is consumer reach. Established channels are converging. Legacies of the old state-run economy continue to thrive and grow. New entrants seek to establish distinct positions in new urban markets and defend those positions. And everyone, it seems, is moving online. Multiple channels to market rule the day, with retailers taking steps to maximize reach but clouding an already complicated, somewhat blurry market picture in the process. There are no hard lines in China, and channels to market are no exception.

With almost half a million retail enterprises, the retail market remains very fragmented.[1] The top 100 retailers in China captured just 11 percent of the country's total retail expenditures in 2010. These retailers have been growing faster than the overall market and therefore taking small steps toward consolidation. In 2010, the top 100 grew more than 21 percent annually, compared with the broader market growth of 16 percent.[2] Although a mature market remains distant, images of consolidation are starting to emerge and will likely accelerate. Figure 5.1 illustrates the small but growing levels of concentration in the market.

The following market forces are likely to result in the continued concentration of retail sales into larger chain-run companies:

- Rising costs in the more established coastal regions are motivating western expansion. These rising costs are primarily driven by increasing wage rates and rising property values.
- Though more moderated, rising costs are being incurred throughout the market, which puts greater emphasis on the scale economies of the larger chains and greater pressure on the individual proprietorships that make up the majority of today's retail landscape.

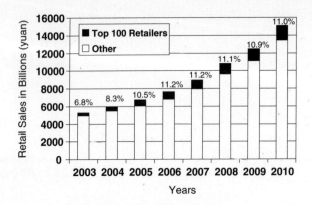

FIGURE 5.1 Growing Concentration in the Retail Sector

Percentages are representative of the market share of total retail spending for the top 100 retailers

Source: Li & Fung Research Centre, "China's Retail Market," June 2011

- Improving infrastructure, as described in Chapter 3, provides the path for countrywide expansion.
- Competition is also fierce in the established coastal economies, providing further impetus for westward expansion.
- Urbanization is increasing and migration to the coastal export manufacturing centers is decreasing.

An Overview of China's Major Channels to Market

There are seven major retail channels driving today's retail market. As Figure 5.2 illustrates, these channels include three channels that are remnants of China's state-run economy as well as new channels that have developed rapidly in recent years.

The first group of market channels are holdovers from the legacy state-run economy. They include department stores, individual single proprietorships (e.g., mom-and-pop stores), and local outdoor markets, commonly referred to as "wet" markets. These legacy channels still exist and play a primary role in how consumers acquire their goods. The government's growing emphasis on improving the safety of the food supply, in addition to consumer preference, is deemphasizing the local, unregulated wet markets in favor of alternatives. Department stores, as described later, suffer from the operating inefficiencies of legacy state-run control. Mom-and-pop stores, while still prevalent, will be increasingly constrained by the rising costs coming into the market.

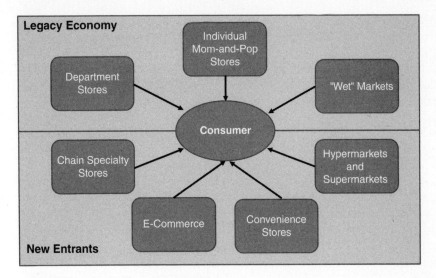

FIGURE 5.2 Channels to a Growing Market

More channels are being added to the market and are capturing a greater share of the consumer's rising purchasing power. Starting with Walmart's entry of the market in 1996, Western retailers pioneered the hypermarket concept in China. Hypermarkets compete with supermarkets for the sale of fast-moving consumer goods. New channels also include specialty stores, comprising the national chains that offer white goods (i.e., appliances and white-fabric articles), electronics, and apparel and the branded stores that target the burgeoning luxury market; convenience stores, with chains rapidly developing in the prosperous coastal cities; and e-commerce, the fastest growing channel today.

Department Stores

Department stores are mainly domestic in origin and are the major channel of distribution for the consumer purchase of apparel, watches, jewelry, and cosmetics. This channel holds a dominant place in the market, with at least 35 of the top 100 retailers. The department store heritage stems from the legacy state-run economy; only two department chains are foreign-owned.

As such, department stores continue to be inexorably tied to the local provincial governments. Their company names are usually recognizable because the province name is often included—for example, Anhui Huishang Group, one of the country's largest retailers; Chongqing General Trading (Group) Company, and Shandong JiaJiaYue Department Store. These companies use favorable ties to their local provincial governments to grow within their respective regions, and they receive preferential treatment in financing, operating licenses, site selection, and government policy.

Department stores are often described as poor merchants. Their typical model, imported from Japan, is that of a concessionaire, in which the department store management leases floor space to companies to sell goods.[3] More than 60 percent of the revenue from the leading department stores comes from this model. For the privilege of the lease, the department stores take a sizable cut, in some cases more than 20 percent of gross sales.

An average of less than a third of total sales in this channel is bought from distributors or directly from manufacturers and merchandised.[4] This dynamic presents multiple challenges for continued growth. Management control over the total shopping experience is limited. The department stores' ability to tailor goods to local consumer tastes is difficult. Although these challenges are recognized, department stores have yet to develop the expertise required to meet them head-on.

These challenges have also made geographic expansion difficult. Perhaps because of their ties with local governments, department stores are in most cases regionally focused, with decentralized operations. A few department store retailers have made inroads outside their home provinces. Beijing Wangfujing Department Stores, for instance, reportedly has stores in 12 provinces. Yet despite the chain's breadth, it operates fewer than 40 stores. Dalian Dashang Group operates 170 stores in 6 provinces. Golden Eagle Retail Group also operates stores in 6 provinces.

Aside from these and a few other exceptions, most department store chains are limited to the home province and perhaps a neighboring province. Like most domestic retailers in other channels, these companies tend to gravitate toward expansion into other formats rather than other locations. Many legacy department stores also operate convenience stores, supermarkets, and shopping malls. With the property boom in the coastal regions, some of these companies have entered the commercial real estate market. Many operate as holding companies, with little operating synergy and scale across their different divisions.

Local Outdoor Markets

One of the major legacy market channels is the local street market, which pervades China's food landscape. The purveyors of modern retail view local food markets as their chief competitors. With no tax, rent, or payroll, the local food market can offer low prices that serve as the market benchmark for comparison.

In addition to having a perceived price advantage, local food markets are embedded in the food culture of China. Most families prepare their meals with fresh food, deemphasizing the importance of packaged foods.

A daily trip to the local market is steeped in the habits and lives of Chinese consumers.

Walmart reportedly sends its managers into wet markets and local stores multiple times a day to check prices in order to remain competitive.[5] Yet there is a growing consensus that local markets are on the wane. Improving consumption safety has become a top government priority, and local markets are difficult to regulate. Consumers too are concerned about food safety and are therefore starting to favor the halls of modern retail shops as a viable alternative.

Hypermarkets

The hypermarket is the new channel that has entered the market in force in the last decade. This channel is dominated by the large Western chains, such as British-centered Tesco, French-owned Carrefour, and U.S.-based Walmart. Taiwan-owned RT-Mart has also entered and expanded its chain of hypermarket stores as well. These companies are the leaders in this channel and have expanded aggressively in the last few years. Unlike some other alternatives in their home markets, hypermarkets tend to be used by more upscale consumers.

In general, their stores are very clean and well-lighted; they have a reputation for and an operational focus on hygiene and cleanliness, compared to the local outdoor markets. Hypermarkets have moved the outdoor wet markets indoors; large portions of the hypermarket store layout is dedicated to live seafood and fresh vegetables with an open-market feel. Alligators, live fish, and frogs are all on display in large bins.

As a result of this change in layout, grocery sales constitute a much higher percentage of overall sales for Chinese hypermarkets than for other types of markets. Opportunities to sample the products pervade the shopping floor. Chinese consumers like to try before they buy, and this preference is readily seen in hypermarkets and other channels.

Chinese consumers have indicated that they often leave a store having bought a different brand than they intended to buy when they entered. Purchasing behavior often breaks away from intent based on the store experience. The greater presence of sample opportunities in these stores and the availability of perishable fresh products are the two main differences between modern China's retail hypermarkets and hypermarket stores in their home markets. In Walmart stores located in China, squid and alligator can be the most prominently displayed food products. Although a hypermarket may be owned by a foreign company, a majority of its merchandise is locally sourced, with an emphasis on fresh foods.

The hypermarket channel is growing to capture a majority share in the grocery sector, accounting for 45 percent of total grocery purchases in the Shanghai market.[6] About 80 percent of all hypermarket sales stem from the large, foreign-owned organizations expanding in the market.[7] Consumers have taken note of the disciplined operations and more consistent high-quality presentation. With the country's consumers spending 14 percent of GDP on food, hypermarkets are poised to benefit.[8] In a market survey in 2005, only 28 percent of consumers stated that hypermarkets were their shopping preference. This increased to 46 percent in 2008, with the increase coming largely at the expense of supermarkets (see Figure 5.3).

Although Walmart claims that its customers shop in its stores an average of more than three times a week, hypermarkets are often viewed as a more occasional shopping destination.[9] You usually need a car to get to one, and there is a mall-like atmosphere to many, with some stores having multiple floors.

Supermarkets

The supermarkets are dominated by domestically owned companies, and their stores are characterized by a more working-class clientele, compared to hypermarkets, and they have a relative lack of Western management methods and modern retail practices. "Stack 'em high" is the prevailing operating practice.

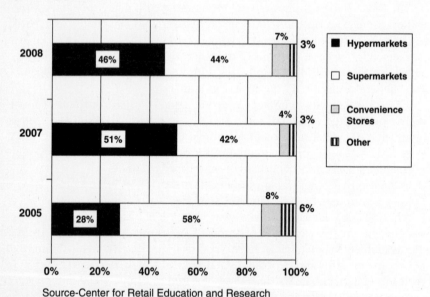

Source-Center for Retail Education and Research

FIGURE 5.3 Increase in Consumer Preference for Hypermarkets

Source: David Miller, "Retail Supply Chain Management," Center for Retail Education and Research, https://site.warrington.ufl.edu/iret/modules-on-retailing-in-china/module-6-retail-supply-chain-management

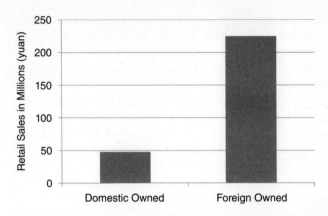

FIGURE 5.4 Sales per Store for the Top 19 Retailers of Fast-Moving Consumer Goods

Data Source: "Selling to Chinese Consumers: Distribution Goes Cutting Edge," HKTDC Research, October 8, 2010, www.hktdc.com

Supermarkets tend to be more price-driven and competitive. In contrast, the Western-owned retailers' management expertise in operating this channel has resulted in much higher revenue and profitability per store, creating a competitive advantage in the market as operational efficiencies become more important. Figure 5.4 compares sales per store, showing the leading, foreign-owned, hypermarket chains compared with their domestically owned rivals.[10]

The domestically owned supermarket companies have greater breadth and market coverage, however, which Figure 5.5 illustrates.

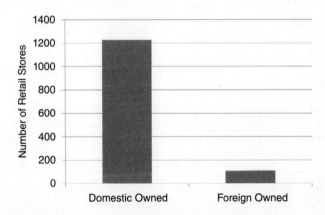

FIGURE 5.5 Average Store Footprint of the Top 19 Retailers for Fast-Moving Consumer Goods

Data Source: "Selling to Chinese Consumers: Distribution Goes Cutting Edge," HKTDC Research, October 8, 2010, www.hktdc.com

These two measures demonstrate the differences within this channel. Largely foreign-owned hypermarkets have fewer stores but dramatically higher sales per store than the domestically owned supermarkets do. Hypermarket stores are more consistent in terms of layout and operations.

A case in point is the supermarket Lianhua. With more than 4,000 stores nationally, this state-owned company is one of the largest retailers in this sector by this measure, and it is much larger in number of stores compared to the foreign-owned hypermarkets. A closer look shows that Lianhua's size is the result of a government-coordinated roll-up of smaller chains. These chains still operate independently and in some cases compete for the same consumers in the same markets. The benefits of scale for China's largest retail chain are yet to emerge.

Within a local market, the hypermarket format has not been able to gain total coverage. Indeed, with new neighborhoods being established almost daily, it seems impossible to keep up with the expansion of big city sprawl. Less than 10 percent of consumers use a car as their transportation for shopping; instead they take public transportation, ride bicycles, or walk.[11] As a result, hypermarkets in their established markets remain inaccessible to many. In response, supermarkets have begun moving up in the market and taking on the target consumer base of hypermarkets.

Supermarkets have also begun to build smaller markets inside residential neighborhoods, providing a closer alternative to the local outdoor markets. Both Walmart and Tesco are responding as well, experimenting with smaller stores closer to residential areas. As urban areas expand, the residential areas are where the competition is growing the fastest.

Convenience Stores

As part of this expansion closer to the point of consumption, domestic chains are also leading the way in the growing channel of convenience stores. While foreign-owned convenience store chains like 7-Eleven have moved into China in recent years, it is the state-owned companies that have gained first-mover advantage, mostly contained within the established metropolitan areas of the coastal regions. The largest domestic supermarket operator, Lianhua, has been quick to deploy its convenience store chain, Quick, across the Shanghai area. The penetration of convenience stores in Shanghai is comparable to the level in cities like New York. Nearly one-third of China's total convenience stores are in the Shanghai market.[12]

The Luxury Channel

In 2010, mainland China was the fifth largest luxury market in the world, with a total market value of close to 10 billion yuan (about USD $1.6 billion). Since the luxury market is growing 27 percent per year, every manufacturer of luxury goods is in it to some extent. Companies like Gucci, Prada, Hermes, and Versace have set up shop and are prepared to stage their next round of growth in the process. Although the luxury market was initially powered by the "big three" cities of Beijing, Shanghai, and Shenzhen, most luxury goods manufacturers have expanded into adjacent and leading provincial capitals like Chongqing, with some companies testing the waters in smaller cities.

Leading the pack in the luxury goods category are watches. Luxury watches constitute more than a quarter of the category's total sales and leading growth rate of 45 percent a year. Watches, cosmetics, and leather goods (e.g., brands like Louis Vuitton and Coach) combined make up almost two-thirds of all luxury-brand sales in the market.

Most of those sales occur in branded stores owned and operated by their respective companies. In a recent survey of luxury consumers, 78 percent reported branded stores as their preferred channel. Luxury-branded companies, as company-owned stores, allow for absolute control of the customer experience to support the brand.

Given this level of influence, site selection of the stores is one of the most vital decisions made by these companies. More geographically and ambitious companies have as many as 70 stores. Coach, for example, has 45 stores. Other companies, perhaps operating with more exclusive products or with a more cautious outlook, have a smaller number of stores. Tiffany & Company, the fine jeweler, has 6 stores and appears largely focused on areas with the largest pools of luxury consumers.

The rise of international tourism, one of China's most coveted luxury "goods," has given rise to a large number of luxury Chinese consumers traveling abroad. The total size of the Chinese luxury market more than doubles when accounting for purchases by Chinese tourists traveling abroad. Bernard Fornas, the president of Cartier International, speaks for all providers of luxury goods in recognizing this trend: "That means we are looking to employ Chinese personnel in our international boutique locations as well as within China. For example, at some of our biggest tourist stores, such as Galleries Lafayette in Paris or Dubai Mall in Dubai, in order to guarantee full service satisfaction, we now ensure a certain proportion of the sales personnel is of Chinese origin."

Continued

A larger challenge for these companies is acquiring the human capital to meet the increasing service demands of their customers. Digital marketing has also arisen as a recent challenge that companies are moving aggressively to meet. Approximately 30 percent of luxury consumers search for information on luxury brands on a weekly basis. The need to engage and interact with consumers in ways that support luxury brands is increasingly important.

The luxury channel will be an increasingly important one to watch, because developments in this market will most likely influence consumer expectations of service, quality, digital engagement, and other areas.

Source: Bain & Company; KPMG

Specialty Stores

Specialty stores—or "category killers," as they have been called—have also made their mark in the market. The most pronounced is the emergence of specialty electronic retailers, led by the domestic companies Gome Electrical Appliances and the Suning Appliance Company. As China's luxury market grows to one of the largest in the global economy, both domestic and foreign-owned branded stores have moved into the market, largely in the eastern third of the country. Toys "R" Us, for example, operates 19 stores in major top-tier cities.[13]

Luxury, another kind of specialty, is almost becoming an additional channel in the market (see sidebar, "The Luxury Channel").

E-Commerce

Online commerce as a channel to market is experiencing dramatic growth. From 2008 to 2012, Li & Fung Research Centre estimates, the ecommerce market rose to capture more than 5 percent of total retail expenditures, an almost fivefold expansion in a four-year period (see Figure 5.6).

The top grossing purely online retailer is the Taobao Group. Established in 2008, the company grew to a revenue base of $30 billion yuan in just four years. With Taobao's nearest rival, a company called 360buy, having little more than one-third the revenue, Taobao dominates this staggering growth channel. The number of online shoppers approached 200 million by the end of 2010, with sales growing more than 30 percent a year.[14] Now Taobao is moving offline as well, establishing its own storefronts.

Meanwhile, the largest retailers have taken notice of the surging online channel, and 34 of the top 100 retailers have embarked on their own online business.[15] As explored in more detail in Chapter 6, China's online shopping

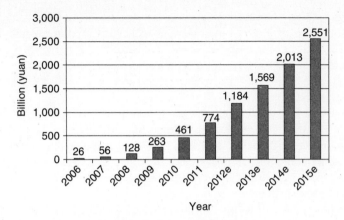

FIGURE 5.6 Growth in the Retail E-Commerce Channel
Lowercase "e" stands for "estimated."
Source: iResearch (www.iresearchchina.com); Slideshare (www.slideshare.net)

market is expected to increase to more than $100 billion in the next two years, clearly changing the retail landscape in the process.[16]

A Closer Look at China's Top Brick-and-Mortar Retailers

A closer look at the largest retailers in China provides a microcosm of how the larger market is evolving. In 2010, the top 10 retailers accounted for more than 780 billion yuan of sales and captured 47 percent of the total retail sales of the top 100.[17] These 10 retailers, and their channels to market, will benefit disproportionately as market consolidation continues. They can be broken down into three categories:

1. The domestic specialty electronics giants of Suning and Gome.
2. The hypermarket leaders. RT-Mart, Walmart, and Carrefour are the foreign-owned hypermarket members in the top 10.
3. The domestic, mostly province-centered, conglomerate retailers. Of these, the Balian group is the largest, which includes the supermarket leader Lianhua.

The two largest retailers in China, the domestic companies Gome and Suning, have come to dominate the robust market for electronics. Gome, formed in the late 1980s, has more than 1,300 stores nationwide, and Suning, formed in the early 1990s, has a comparable number of stores. Both chains have experienced dramatic year-to-year growth rates of more than

30 percent. Gome currently accrues about one-fourth of its revenues from middle-tier cities.[18] Both companies are examples of domestically owned companies that have established a national distribution network. These two companies make up a channel that has acted as a "market maker" for the manufacturers of personal computers, television sets, appliances, and other electronic goods.

In the last few years, foreign-owned hypermarkets have expanded dramatically. RT-Mart, Carrefour, and Walmart are the only foreign-owned companies that have established themselves in the top 10 chains. Walmart now has 306 supercenters in 25 provinces and serves as a case study of how the retail market is evolving. Figure 5.7 highlights the number of supercenters in each Chinese province.

Another way to view the current distribution of Walmart supercenters is by the demand cluster analysis (described in Chapter 4) shown in Table 5.1.

Walmart's store distribution demonstrates many of the insights from the consumer economic analysis presented in Chapter 4. More than 20 percent of Walmart's stores are in Guangdong province, where population density and discretionary incomes are the highest. That region was also Walmart's point of entry to the market; its first phase of stores were located there. The company's current store distribution is also an indication of where the fastest market growth is likely to occur in the future.

The Anhui demand cluster contains 65 supercenters. Of these, 13 are in Hefei, the capital city of the Anhui province. This province, with its high population density, one of the highest income growth rates, and its large population, is leading the way in the next phase of China's growth markets.

Also leading the way are two provinces in the Chengdu demand cluster: Yunnan, with 16 stores, the majority in its capital city, Kunming; and Chongqing, with 14 stores. Also notable in Walmart's current absence in the far western provinces, such as Gansu, Qinghai, Tibet, and Xinjiang. These provinces, with low population density and flatter income growth, do not appear to be on the company's immediate investment horizons.

Walmart's expansion is a sign of the emerging importance of operating and supply chain efficiencies. In early 2010, Walmart announced that it was establishing global merchandising centers, with the goal of procuring 60 to 70 percent of its products directly from the manufacturers. Although that goal has fallen short because of the continued challenges of cross-province transportation and coordination, Walmart and other hypermarket retailers are pioneering the market in this direction.[19]

In addition to these sites, Walmart and other hypermarket retailers have begun experimenting with smaller formats, both convenience stores and neighborhood markets, in Shenzhen. As supercenters continue to act as a foothold for expansion in the inland areas of the market, format innovation helps the company to increase its coverage of local markets.

Locations of Walmart Supercenters

FIGURE 5.7 Location of Walmart Supercenters

Source: Walmart

TABLE 5.1 Location of Walmart Supercenters by Demand Cluster

Demand Cluster / Province	Number of Supercenters	Demand Cluster / Province	Number of Supercenters
Anhui Demand Cluster	**65**	**Beijing Demand Cluster**	**66**
Anhui	13	Beijing	10
Henan	5	Hebei	2
Hubei	14	Heilongjiang	10
Hunan	13	Inner Mongolia	1
Jiangsu	20	Jilin	7
		Liaoning	13
		Shandong	13
		Shanxi	6
		Tianjin	4

Demand Cluster / Province	Number of Supercenters	Demand Cluster / Province	Number of Supercenters
Chengdu Demand Cluster	**54**	**Guangdong Demand Cluster**	**122**
Chongqing	14	Fujian	19
	8	Guangdong	59
Shaanxi	4	Guangxi	4
Sichuan	12	Jiangxi	10
Yunnan	16	Shanghai	12
Gansu	0	Zhejiang	17
Ningxia	0	Hainan	0
Qinghai	0	Guangxi	0
Tibet	0		
Xinjiang	0		

Like every large retailer in China, Walmart is moving online. In February 2012, the company announced that it intends to take a majority stake in Yihaodian, one of the country's largest online superstores.[20] One of the significant benefits of this increased investment in online commerce is greater access to local markets. Yihaodian offers next-day delivery service for its main markets, with logistical centers in Beijing, Shanghai, and Guangzhou.[21]

By combining Yihaodian's operations with its physical stores, Walmart will quickly be able to deploy a "bricks-and-clicks" retail model, enabling consumers to order and pick up in-store, return in-store, or reach additional consumers outside its current store coverage in areas with Yihaodian's established delivery network. That same model can then be migrated west to the regions with established supercenters to serve as a growth platform for the company.

Everyone, it seems, is everywhere. Department stores continue to use their government relationships to deepen their strengths in their home provinces. Hypermarkets are expanding nationally and bringing a consistent, high-quality, customer experience with increasing scale. Their competitors are responding by going deeper into local markets with neighborhood and convenience stores. There's a rush to catch the online marketplace.

Table 5.2 provides a summary of the major channels operating in today's retail market.

TABLE 5.2 Summary of China's Major Retail Channels

Type	Channel	Leading Players	Market Dynamics
Legacy	Department stores	Dalian Dashang Group Co., Ltd.	Total market: $250 billion yuan (or about USD $40 billion).[22]
		Beijing Wangfujing Department Store (Group) Co., Ltd.	Regionally focused in home provinces.
		Golden Eagle Retail Group Ltd.	Primary revenue stream through concessionary model.
		Intime Department Store (Group), Co., Ltd.	Challenged to develop modern merchandising capabilities.
			Prime locations and advantages through local government influence.
			Multichannel operators and moving aggressively online.
New entrants	Hypermarkets and supermarkets	Walmart RT-Mart Carrefour A Best Trust Mart Yonghui Tesco Lotte Lotus Auchan	Hypermarkets attract upscale consumers.
			Traditional open markets as the largest competition.
		These are the 10 largest supermarket and hypermarket retailers.[23]	Greater emphasis on grocery items and fresh foods.
		(Note: Walmart holds a large equity stake in the Trust Mart chain.)	Companies moving inside residential areas with a smaller distribution of stores.

(continued)

Type	Channel	Leading Players	Market Dynamics
	E-commerce	Taobao 360buy Joyo Amazon Dangdang Vancl Newegg Redbaby M18 Suning Yihaodian These are the top 10 purely e-commerce companies.	Total market: 498 billion yuan (or about USD $80 billion).[24] Leading players (top 10): 53.7 billion yuan (or about USD $8.6 billion).[25] Online sales booming. Taobao undisputed leader with close to three times the revenue of 360buy, which is number two in the market. Group buying huge source of growth.
	Convenience stores	Meiyijia Convenience Store Quick (Lianhua) Alldays, Kedi (NGS Supermarket Group) Tianfu Sun High Sichuan Huhui Business Group Suguo Supermarket Company Shanxi Taiyuan Tangjiu Supermarket Company	Market entry a relatively recent focus by chains. Largely domestic, with some foreign players, like 7-Eleven, also present. Currently relegated mostly to the coastal areas. Shanghai holds one-third of the total number of convenience stores in the market.
	Specialty stores	Gome Suning Best Buy Hisap High Technology Corporation	Category led by domestic players. Extensive national network. Poised for greater expansion.

From a small base, modern retailing is fast emerging to accelerate China's consumer economy. The foreign-owned hypermarket chains long ago entered the market and in more recent years have marched westward to establish stores in most of the country's inland provinces. As they do, legacy department stores and domestic retailers are responding with new strategies.

How will these market channels evolve? What does the future go-to-market model look like in the Chinese market? Unlike more mature economies with established infrastructures, China depends on the supply chain of these companies and their suppliers. What is the current state of distribution capabilities? Are they keeping up with westward expansion? Can they deliver in the more demanding environments in the smaller formats? While the market consolidates, mapping current distribution capabilities and trends will help us determine the answers to those questions and chart a new, emerging retail model for the market.

This is what subsequent chapters will cover. First, however, the next chapter will discuss the arena where most Chinese consumers start their shopping: online, immersed in a dynamic, fast-growing, collaborative, and unique digital world.

Notes

1. Thomas White, *BRIC Spotlight Report*, "Retail Sector in China: The Next Big Thing?" June 2011, www.thomaswhite.com/pdf/bric-spotlight-report-china-retail-june-11.pdf.

2. Li & Fung Research Centre, "China's Retail Market," June 2011, www.funggroup.com/eng/knowledge/research/china_dis_issue85.pdf.

3. Ira Kalish, "China's Consumer Market: What Next?" Deloitte Research, 2009, www.deloitte.com/assets/Dcom-MiddleEast/Local%20Assets/Documents/Industries/Consumer%20Business/me_consumer_business_china_consumer_report_09.pdf.

4. Li & Fung Research Centre, "Department Stores in China," August 2011, www.funggroup.com/eng/knowledge/research/china_dis_issue89.pdf.

5. Kalish, "China's Consumer Market.

6. Ibid.

7. Alan Hallman, "Spending on Food Surges While Distribution Remains a Challenge," *Global Agriculture Information Network Report*, U.S. Department of Agriculture Foreign Agriculture Service, January 15, 2010. http://gain.fas.usda.gov/Recent%20GAIN%20Publications/RETAIL%20FOOD%20SECTOR_Shanghai%20ATO_China%20-%20Peoples%20Republic%20of_12-2-2009.pdf.

8. "Grocer's Green," *Economist*, April 10, 2012, www.economist.com/blogs/graphicdetail/2012/04/daily-chart-3.

9. Kalish, "China's Consumer Market.

10. "Selling to Chinese Consumers: Distribution Goes Cutting Edge," HKTDC Research, October 8, 2010, www.hktdc.com.

11. David Miller, "Retail Supply Chain Management," Center for Retail Education and Research, https://site.warrington.ufl.edu/iret/modules-on-retailing-in-china/module-6-retail-supply-chain-management.

12. Hallman, "Spending on Food Surges While Distribution Remains a Challenge."

13. "Selling to Chinese Consumers."

14. White, *BRIC Spotlight Report*.

15. Li & Fung, "China's Retail Market."

16. "Wal-Mart Ups Stake in China E-Commerce," *Wall Street Journal*, February 2012.

17. "China Power of Retailing," Deloitte, 2011, www.deloitte.com/assets/Dcom-China/Local%20Assets/Documents/Industries/Consumer%20business%20and%20transportation/cn_cbt_ChinaPowersRetailing2011_181011.pdf.

18. White, *BRIC Spotlight Report*.

19. "Selling to Chinese Consumers."

20. "Walmart Global eCommerce Completes Increased Investment in Yihaodian," Walmart press release, October 26, 2012, http://news.walmart.com/news-archive/2012/10/26/walmart-global-ecommerce-completes-increased-investment-in-yihaodian.

21. "Wal-Mart's Investments in Chinese E-Commerce Market," MSN Money, February 22, 2012, http://money.msn.com/top-stocks/post.aspx?post=d3f73abe-ed6e-440e-82b9-e85a104427a9.

22. Li & Fung, "Department Stores in China."

23. "China Power of Retailing," Deloitte.

24. Hu Haiyan, "China Daily Europe: Enduring Commitment to Succeed," August 19, 2011, http://europe.chinadaily.com.cn/epaper/2011-08/19/content_13151490.htm.

25. Li & Fung Research Centre," China's Online Retailing Market, 2011," October 2011, www.funggroup.com/eng/knowledge/research/china_dis_issue90.pdf.

CHAPTER 6

Guan Xi Goes Online

Zŏuhòumén means "in through the back door." That term encapsulates the survival method used by today's grandparents in China during their younger years. During the days of the political campaigns led by Chairman Mao, the government apparatus controlled all aspects of life, and people who were indebted to you could be called on to help. *Guan xi* is the Chinese term for this phenomenon. Perhaps the use of a connection and a debt repaid would get you a break in the monthly food ration or continued job security among the ever-watching eyes of the work unit (*dan wei*).

During the political upheavals of the Cultural Revolution, past affiliations, such as a university education, were kept hidden. Parents exchanged favors with those in positions of influence to keep their children from being sent to the countryside in what were then labor camps in all but name. In the earlier Chinese eras of draconian state control, bypassing bureaucratic intransigence meant using the powers of social connection steeped in trust and obligation. Using *guan xi*, connections, to go *zŏuhòumén*, in through the back door, became the central organizing premise of an informal underground society. Having good *guan xi*, a vast network of connections to call in favors to, often made the difference in stark survival terms.

Guan xi has always been part of Chinese society. Confucian thought is steeped in the sense of reciprocal obligation in the practice of generosity. *The Book of Rites*, one of the five classic books of Confucian thought, outlines reciprocity as a central tenet in a civil society. "What the rules of propriety value is that of reciprocity. . . . All sources and roots of disaster and disorder come from failure in returning grace."[1]

This notion of reciprocity runs deep. On a personal level, the bonds between individuals and between families are formed through it. The bond between two individuals, extended across one's full set of relationships, is the starting point for understanding *guan xi*. A sense of mutual obligation, dependence, trust, and indebtedness, which can hold throughout lifetimes and even across generations, are at its core.

These bonds and expanding networks operated in the fabric of society during the lean years of Communist rule after the revolution. The practice of *guan xi* flourished as the main vehicle by which people could secure resources in a scarce society and subvert the politicized allocation of those resources through the established government-run channels. *Guan xi*'s cultural history and widespread practice made it a central tenet society's functioning. Informal networks, developed and maintained secretly and away from prying eyes, were how things got done.

Today, the term *guan xi* is used often and is considered by many to be cliché. The Chinese, as well as experts in Chinese culture, decry its frequent use. Indeed, the term is mentioned repeatedly as an entry point for Western understanding of Chinese culture. It is used too much as an umbrella term. Others use the term to credential themselves: "having *guan xi*" means you are connected and is intended to send a message that expert navigation through the ambiguous world of China can be had for a price. No doubt this happens.

Leading academics have suggested that the practice of *guan xi* is coming to end. As China makes advances in the rule of law and as market mechanisms start to have greater sway, it is argued, the need for *guan xi* and the motivations for employing it are ebbing. The market emphasizes action away from personal favors and toward maximizing profit—that's how the thinking goes.

Zŏuhòumén, "in through the back door," has also fallen out of favor in today's China. The practice implies that institutional shortcuts off to the side give credence to corruption in the eyes of many. Personal favors, conducted between individuals outside the glare of institutions and law, do indeed have the potential to breed corrupt practice, but indications are that corruption remains a corrosive part of Chinese life. As Chinese law becomes more transparent, these practices may fade and with it, the practices of *guan xi* and *zŏuhòumén*.[2]

Or so the argument goes. Legal frameworks are indeed developing. Today's young middle-class Chinese have no memory of the survival skills practiced by their forebears through *guan xi*. Despite this, the cultural roots of *guan xi*—making connections of trust independent of established institutions—remain present.

Enter the Internet. The ability to make social connections is now online and scaled well beyond one's immediate social circle. The ability to reference a product, seek out independent voices on news and culture, and offer opinions is now operating on a grand scale. In that light, *guan xi* is alive and kicking online. It's not your parents or grandparents' *guan xi*, however.

While the historical practice of *guan xi* may be on the wane, it is still essential for companies to know its underlying themes in order to understand today's consumers, how they interact with emerging brands, and how companies can reach them. Knowing the historical context of *guan xi* is a useful way to understand how different Internet usage is among Chinese consumers and how to interact and reach them.

An Overview of China's Digital World

The size of China's digital world is staggering. No other country comes close to China's current Internet population of 513 million users. China's Internet population is more than twice that of the United States, which has an Internet population of 245 million, and more than four times that of India, which has an Internet population of 121 million. All other countries fall below 100 million, only one-fifth the size of China's number of users today.[3] Even though China's user base already dwarfs that of every other country, its growth rate continues; today's Internet usage in China is still in its formative stages.

Almost half of China's users, 215 million, came online between 2008 and 2011, just as many users came online in this short amount of time in the United States. Total penetration remains lower than in most other markets—around 40 percent—yet access costs are much lower than in other countries. Broadband is available to 90 percent of the Chinese population for only $10 per month, which is less than half the access cost in other emerging economies, like Brazil and India.[4]

As China's Internet has quickly blossomed, new companies have emerged and become powerhouses. China's Internet is led by different companies than in other markets, as illustrated in Table 6.1. These companies form the "big four" leaders of China's Internet landscape.

Baidu was formed in 2000 and is therefore only a little more than a decade old. With more than $2.5 billion in annual sales and a market capitalization of more than $41 billion, Baidu is one of the most formidable Internet companies in China.[5] Its focus is web searches, with the huge

TABLE 6.1 China's Internet Leaders

Function	Leader in Rest of the World	China's Leader
Search	Google	Baidu
Commerce	Amazon	Taobao (Alibaba)
Social Media	Facebook	Tencent (QQ, Qzone) Sina Weibo

majority in China going through its platform. Estimates indicate that Baidu owns close to 80 percent of all China-emanated web searches.[6] Like its Western counterpart Google, Baidu has a business of selling search-based advertising. It recently announced its intentions to launch a smartphone in China using its own platform and to branch out into other areas like social networking.[7]

The consumer e-commerce market in China is dominated by Taobao (www.taobao.com). Established in 2008 by Jack Ma, Taobao is the leading online retailer in China by any measure. In the consumer-to-consumer market (like eBay), Taobao has an estimated 90 percent market share. It has achieved nearly 50 percent market share for all business-to-consumer transactions. Of the leading e-commerce companies in China, no other company comes close to Taobao's market awareness and revenue, which is three times more than that of the nearest company.

Tencent's instant messaging platform, QQ, its complementary social media platform Qzone, and its microblogging sites are the leading social media applications for China's users. Qzone has more than 500 million users. Tencent, established in 1998, is the oldest of China's big four Internet companies. According to company reports, more than 140 million people can be found online simultaneously using QQ.[8] This has been driven in part by the company's aggressive entry of mobile platforms; it launched its mobile chat service in 2011.[9] The company reported that its valuation is more than 80 times its annual revenue currently exceeding $6 billion.[10]

With a market capitalization close to $50 billion, Tencent, like its search counterpart Baidu, is one of the most highly valued Internet companies in the world. Sina Weibo (literally, "Sina Microblog") was launched in 2009 and is quickly rising to leadership status, with more than 30 percent of Internet users registered with the service. About 100 million messages are posted daily on the platform. The difference between these two competing services is customer demographics. There is certainly lots of overlap, yet Tencent appears to have stronger penetration in the middle-tier and inland areas while Sina Weibo appeals to more upscale users.

As in other parts of the world, the Internet in China has become mobile. China has 1 billion mobile phone subscribers—more mobile phone subscribers than landline users. Consumers are increasingly using mobile devices for communication, Internet access, and information. The big four leaders in China's Internet market are increasingly moving into mobile platforms to take advantage of them.

As growth in Internet usage continues apace, it is becoming a centralizing function for the Chinese. More than other markets, the Chinese have embraced the Internet as a way to connect, communicate, consume, contribute, and buy.

The E-Commerce Rocket

Approximately 30 million people in China are expected to shop online for the first time each year between now and 2015.[11] An additional 148 million people have already been using the Internet for shopping since mid-2010.[12] In the span of just a few years, the online channel is approaching the same level of market share that it took brick-and-mortar retailers several years to reach. One government body estimates that China's online retailing market already accounts for 5 percent of total retail sales in the market. With spending levels increasing and total online sales growing at a rate of 60 to 80 percent a year, it will only be a short time before online retailing is the largest channel to consumers in the market. As the *Economist* stated, "The future of e-commerce is Chinese."[13]

Recent estimates from the China-based market research firm iResearch show the tremendous growth. In 2008, online shopping sales totaled less than 130 billion yuan (about USD $21 billion). That number increased more than sixfold through 2011, with reported sales at 770 billion yuan (about USD $124 billion), and estimates are that sales will increase beyond 2,550 billion yuan (about USD $410 billion) by the year 2015.[14]

A small set of e-commerce giants are riding the wave of this phenomenal growth, with the top 10 e-commerce companies capturing close to 80 percent of total sales in the market. This level of concentration in other retail channels is rare, and it demonstrates how a handful of companies have exploited this new market.

For branded manufacturers, there are advantages to this consolidation in reaching consumers: greater breadth of market coverage, much higher growth rates, and a greater share of total retail sales. By the end of 2011, online sales reportedly accounted for 4.5 to 5 percent of total retail sales. Most of those sales were transacted on the small set of the country's 10 leading online retailers.

Contrast this to China's offline retailing world, and the benefits of greater reach can be seen. In the offline retailing world, the top 100 retailers captured 11 percent of total sales. But the offline world is much more complex, containing a vast mix of state-run entities and foreign enterprises and retailers, with regional focus existing alongside national distribution. And the offline retailers are growing more slowly. Granted, the top 100 offline retailers are growing around 18 percent a year. Most are growing as fast as they can build stores and move online themselves. But online e-commerce sales are growing many times faster (see Figure 6.1).

Amid the small group of e-commerce leaders, Alibaba's Taobao is the undisputed leader. Founded in 2008, the company controls almost half of all consumer Internet purchases.

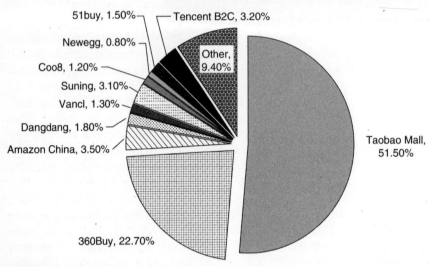

B2C Market Share (2012, First Quarter)

51buy, 1.50% — Tencent B2C, 3.20%

Newegg, 0.80%

Coo8, 1.20%

Other, 9.40%

Suning, 3.10%

Vancl, 1.30%

Dangdang, 1.80%

Amazon China, 3.50%

Taobao Mall, 51.50%

360Buy, 22.70%

FIGURE 6.1 China's E-Commerce Leaders

Source: iResearch Consulting Group, Q1 2012 China E-Commerce Report, www.iresearchchina.com/samplereports/4148.html.

A few statistics illustrate the scale of Tmall, Taobao's recently established commerce platform:

- 30,000 brands are represented.[15]
- In just one month, November 2011, Taobao sold $817 million worth of products.
- Taobao sells an average of 48,000 items *every minute.*[16]

Taobao's parent company, Alibaba, continues to pursue a strategy of targeting continued dominance in the market. Its pay service, Alipay, is China's leading online payment platform. Roughly equivalent to the Western world's PayPal, Alipay has more than 600 million registered users and processes at least 11 million transactions per day.[17] Tmall has initiated multiple partnerships with other e-commerce leaders to minimize competition. Because Taobao's sites are cut off from Baidu's search engines, consumers have become increasingly accustomed to using Taobao as their portal for all things concerning online shopping.

Given Taobao's immense scale, competitors are hoping that a more narrow focus with an improved customer experience will help them to differentiate and gain market share. It will be challenging for them, given

Taobao's dominant position. Yet there should be room for additional competitors to thrive, given the substantial growth rates.

Why are consumers rushing to the online market? The first reason is price. More than 50 percent of consumers say they shop online because they can get a better price than in offline stores. Online discounting feeds this trend. With inefficient supply chains, excessive inventories are a fact of life in China. This merchandise has found a home in online discounts. The second reason is selection: consumers state that a wider selection of goods, including items available only online, is a critical motivational factor. Convenience of delivery is the third reason. Thus price, product availability, and convenience operate as the value proposition cornerstones for the online marketplace.

Online shoppers, most of them under the age of 30, are predominantly buying shoes, clothing, and leather goods online. Other durable items—like books, videos, digital electronics, and cosmetics—are also at the top of the list. Yet even though these items represent the most in-demand categories today, more and more categories are moving into the online market. The company 360buy, one of the e-commerce leaders in today's market, was originally known for consumer electronics and has recently expanded into food and baby products.[18] Another leader, Dangdang, started out in the e-commerce category of books and is now expanding into cosmetics, clothing, and electronics.

Both brick-and-mortar stores and an online presence are increasingly seen as required and as operating in tandem. More traditional retailers are investing their way into the e-commerce world. Walmart's previously mentioned investment in Yihaodian is one example. Another is Gome's execution of a controlling stake investment in COO8, one of the leading e-commerce platforms, in 2010. And Taobao is setting up an offline store network.

Many consumers have stated a preference for viewing product information online before visiting a store and for comparing prices from their store visits online. A study by the Boston Consulting Group found that more than 50 percent of consumers visit a brick-and-mortar retailer before purchasing online. These characteristics—the integration of online and offline channels and the practice of buying online and picking up in-store—are working their way into today's retail environments.

One of the reasons the e-commerce market is growing so remarkably is its ready access to consumers who lack easily accessible alternatives to offline stores. In more developed markets, the rise of online e-commerce was predicated in part by large investments in initial consumer trials of a different purchase path. Consumers, trained in the "touch and feel" way of going to a store, had to reorient their purchase behavior in order to become more accustomed to online purchasing. That took investments and a willingness to absorb higher customer acquisition costs.

These costs are lower in China simply because brick-and-mortar modern retail has yet to arrive in many parts of the country. In the established top-tier cities like Shanghai, consumers are moving farther away from the central commercial districts to escape skyrocketing real estate prices. These cities are expanding beyond retailers' established formats. In the capitals of the inland provinces, it can take consumers hours on public transportation to cross the metropolitan areas.

So even with a number of retail stores, retailers—and the consumers they seek—find market coverage and accessibility to be a challenge. The widely available Internet often provides a quicker and easier alternative, given the lack of brick-and-mortar retail. The implication for consumer-focused companies is that much of the consumer population increasingly perceives online retail to be the primary channel for purchase. If a retailer is not there today, it risks losing market share tomorrow. This is also a risk for retailers who fear disintermediation (the elimination of an intermediary—in this case, the salesperson—in a transaction). E-commerce's consolidated channel and broad market coverage could mean higher returns for branded manufacturers through investments in the online channel.

E-Logistics: The New Core Capability

One of the drivers fueling the growth in e-commerce is the low cost of package shipment in China. E-commerce firms have taken advantage of the state-subsidized shipping industry, which provides countrywide coverage at cheap rates. Estimates are that from 50 to 80 percent of all packages on the road in China come from orders on Taobao's web site.

Many e-commerce operators employ third-party delivery companies, especially in bottom-tier cities and the inland provinces. While these delivery companies have benefited enormously, their reliability varies considerably. Consumers may be concerned, and rightfully so, that brand goods purchased through a reliable e-commerce company are swapped for fake goods in the delivery process. Goods are also dropped and broken. Because of these challenges, e-commerce companies are increasingly looking at building their own distribution capabilities to cover last-mile delivery. Alibaba, the parent company of Taobao, is investing 25 billion yuan to build its own distribution and delivery networks.[19]

The leading e-commerce companies understand that last-mile delivery is a core capability of its value proposition for customers, for convenient and reliable access to products, and for products unavailable to brick-and-mortar alternatives. One thing is clear: e-commerce companies are not sitting still. They recognize that greater distribution aligns with this value proposition and is a foundation of their growth strategy. They are building distribution networks rivaling any of those operating in the market today.

Even with greater distribution capabilities coming online, e-commerce companies will need to continue relying on third parties in some areas of the market. Steps are being taken to provide greater customer assurance about their use. Through Alipay, the online payment mechanism used for 50 percent of e-commerce purchases, payment is not processed until delivery is complete. E-commerce leaders are providing greater training in delivery and customer services. In some cases, uniforms are required to be worn as a sign of affiliation with the e-commerce company and to enhance consumer trust.

The use of third parties and company-owned distribution networks will probably coexist in the foreseeable future. With product demand soaring and extending to every part of the country, e-commerce companies are using every asset available to maximize consumer reach and growth.

The Influence of Social Media

Social media have had a greater influence on consumer purchases in China than anywhere else on the planet. It is the grease that moves the wheels of a consumer's purchase decision. China's social media universe is where consumers connect with others and search for trusted reviews of product information outside official sources. Social media's influence on consumer purchase and brand equity is perhaps the most defining difference between China's consumer market and markets elsewhere. China is by far the most active social media market, with a much greater usage that extends across more platforms than that of other markets.

The king of social media is Tencent, one of the "big four" of China's current Internet landscape. Its Internet messaging platform, QQ, is the stuff of legend. Though the leader, Tencent is just one of an increasingly crowded set of social media applications. The previously mentioned Sina Weibo is one of China's leading microblogging sites, with 250 million registered users.[20] When an event of significance happens in China that people want to know about, they eschew official media outlets and seek more trustworthy information through outlets like Sina. Renren, with 137 million registered users, is mainly composed of college students. Given the younger demographic profile of its users, Renren has many social media innovations. Table 6.2 outlines the market's leaders.

With many providers, social media are being embraced in China. The difference in the application of social media is cultural. In the past, the concept of *guan xi* was applied to the connections made between people bound by trust and the exchange of favors for the purpose of surviving bureaucratic institutions. Today, the same principles are applied online in China's digital world.

TABLE 6.2 China's Leading Social Media Platforms

Platform	Registered Users (in millions)	Primary User Profile	Percent of Consumers Listing It as Their Favorite
Qzone (Tencent)	536	Broad base	44
Tencent Weibo	310	Smaller city base	8
Sina Weibo	250	Upscale and urban base	19
RenRen	137	College students	19
Kaixin	116	White-collar workers	7

Source: We Are Social, McKinsey & Co.

As an indication of how much consumers trust data from companies about their own products, only 19 percent of consumers visit the official online sites of individual brands. This contrasts with more than 40 percent in other countries, like Japan and the United States.[21] Where do all of China's other millions of users go instead? They are on platforms like Sina Weibo, comparing notes. More than 80 percent of Chinese youth check online comments before making a purchase decision.

And they are not just consumers of this information. Chinese web users contribute content—comments, microblog postings, and reviews—at more than twice the rate of social media users in the United States.[22] In many cases, users contribute and consume information anonymously. People who post on the Chinese Internet cherish their anonymity more than people in other markets, and this provides a freer exchange of ideas. In Western markets, Internet users view their online lives as more of an extension of their offline lives. In China, greater anonymity creates a more defined, expressive, open, and separate culture.

The overall objectives of social media in China are similar to those in other markets. These objectives include the ability to promote the intended brand characteristics by generating and influencing conversations about them. The objectives also include the ability to promote positive consumer associations that saturate the web presence. Online, a company can better control the message if it fills the space.

Sina Weibo is quickly becoming the brand portal for Chinese social media, especially for luxury goods. As more and more luxury-brand providers are being pulled into social media by consumers, the providers' first step is to deploying a brand-centered web site using Sina. The second step is to initiate promotional campaigns to generate consumer awareness. An example of an often used promotion is a series of videos put on Youku

Who Are the Leaders in Online Engagement?

What's a good way to measure social media's level of engagement with consumers? Social media in China are used differently and distinctively from their use in other countries. Distinctive usage requires a distinctive evaluation method.

L2, a social media research house, evaluates a firm's level of online social engagement using a weighted index composed of four factors:

1. **Effectiveness of the web site.** This criterion includes content functionality, localization, and cultural relevance. This factor is weighted 40 percent and is the most influential on overall score. A great promotion will perform poorly without a web destination that catches people's attention.
2. **Search engine optimization.** This criterion is weighted 25 percent. It covers the likely traffic to the Chinese site, the traffic from China to the global site, and favorable search results through Baidu.
3. **Favorable content and overall brand presence.** This criterion, measured across the major social media applications (RenRen, Qzone, Youku, and Kaixin001) makes up 20 percent of the overall score.
4. **Digital marketing coverage.** This criterion delivers 15 percent of the total score. It comprises a company's activities in e-mail marketing, blog posts, and activities on bulletin board system sites.

Based on L2's scoring system, here are the 10 best companies at engaging consumers in China's digital world:

1. Lancôme
2. BMW
3. Estée Lauder
4. Audi
5. Clinique
6. Mercedes-Benz
7. Clarins
8. Acura
9. Cadillac
10. Wuliangye (the only Chinese brand on the list)

Note that this list is composed entirely of luxury auto and skin-care product companies. These categories represent the leaders in online social engagement. Luxury jewelers like Tiffany and fashion companies like Gucci are in the next tier of rankings and have made great strides to improve their ratings since the index was released.

Source: L2 Digital IQ Index, L2

(the Chinese version of YouTube). Documentaries are put on the web and reviewed by influential bloggers, and stores use web-based promotions for their events.

In China, it's important to consolidate consumer conversations, and Sina Weibo is increasingly the channel that is used to do so. As promotions generate high levels of awareness, more and more consumers are pulled into the brand's established web presence and begin interacting. As this interaction increases, a sense of community is formed, and consumer-to-consumer interactions begin. Although these interactions are difficult to control, they take place within the context of company-designed messaging and branded sites, so the influence is established and present.

As consumers come into the community, more opportunities emerge for branded companies to reach their most fervent advocates and most demanding consumers. Promotion turns into conversation, and conversation turns into community, which then translates to higher purchase rates and greater brand equity.[23]

Luxury automobile manufacturers were the first to establish online communities in China's digital world. Mercedes, BMW, and Cadillac reportedly have more than 200,000 followers each on their established sites, using Sina Weibo. They are among the highest-rated companies for digital engagement in the market. Clothing markets are rising fast in their levels of sophistication. Burberry established more than 120,000 followers in the first few months after its deployment of a Sina Weibo web site (see sidebar, "Who Are the Leaders in Online Engagement?" which rates companies on their digital engagement).

An example of an integrated marketing campaign was executed by the Diageo-owned brand Johnny Walker. Diageo designed a web-based promotion with two basic thrusts. First, the company teamed with Han Han, who, with an estimated following of 300 million, is one of China's most popular bloggers. Diageo's ability to strike this partnership was no doubt the key to getting ready access to a large audience for the promotion.[24]

Second, using this influential blog, Diageo developed a unique set of media dubbed the Yulu Documentaries to build brand awareness, influence users, and increase traffic. The subject matter of the films was overcoming adversity. Given what we have learned about the historical instability of China, this subject matter strikes at the heart of many Chinese consumers. Traffic mushroomed, and the campaign generated 20 million video viewings in just eight weeks. Perhaps more important, consumers seeking information on Diageo and its brands through Baidu or other formats (remember, consumers in China do this far more than consumers in any other market) were likely to be directed to these sites as a result of the search returns and promotion-generated content.[25]

Before Apple's iTunes, there was Napster, a large, ungoverned destination for pirated music sustained by a community of users. China's social media universe is a bit like that, except that the exchange is not music but opinions, style, fashion, and culture. The Chinese online social networks are deeper and more peer-operated than elsewhere. This is where consumer-focused companies need to start in reaching consumers.

Given the dramatic differences between China and other countries in terms of social media, Chinese consumers expect to be engaged up front and online in the purchasing process. At the same time that consumers expect brands to have a social media presence, they also look for independent views on multiple social networking platforms. Being active and influencing this process is paramount in reaching Chinese consumers.

Go Where the People Are

As China's consumer market develops, consumers can be found in an active, thriving online digital world. This world discovers and spreads the word on new products, defines trends in fashion, and embraces youth culture. It also provides independent and authoritative voices on products and services.

Enabled by widespread Internet access, the growth rates of e-commerce are eclipsing those of other modern retail channels. Those other, brick-and-mortar channels simply cannot expand fast enough to catch up with the coverage and product breadth of the e-commerce alternative. As a result, e-commerce will continue to have an outsized influence on consumer reach in China's market than in countries with more developed brick-and-mortar retail channels.

Accessible to consumers, the e-commerce channel is also readily accessible to consumer-focused companies. Consolidated into a small set of leading domestic companies, these brand companies can begin to tap into this growing channel and reach many more consumers with less investment, compared to other alternatives. These companies need to engage consumers directly through social media and China's unique digital world, developing consumer awareness where consumers search for it. We now know where consumers are doing this. They are online.

Notes

1. Jin Guan, "*GuanxXi*: The Key to Achieving Success in China," *Sino-Platonic Papers*, December 2011.

2. Douglas Guthrie, "The Declining Significance of *Guan Xi* in China's Economic Transition," *China Quarterly,* June 1998.

3. Mary Meeker, "Internet Trends," *Internet World Statistics*, May 30, 2012; www.internetworldstats.com/top20.htm.

4. Jeff Walters, Youchi Kuo, Waldemar Jap, and Hubert Hsu, "The World's Next E-Commerce Superpower: Navigating China's Unique Online-Shopping Ecosystem," Boston Consulting Group, November 2011.

5. "Baidu Profile," Finance, www.finance.yahoo.com.

6. Leo Sun, "Baidu (BIDU) Claims 75.5% of China's Search Market As Google Continues to Slide," *Investor Guide*, January 27, 2011, www.investorguide.com/article/7667/baidu-bidu-claims-75-5-of-chinas-search-market-as-google-continues-to-slide.

7. Ingrid Lundgren, "Baidu Q2 Sales Up 60% to $859M, Almost All Down to Search; Focus Is on Mobile and Cloud Ahead," Tech Crunch, July 23, 2012, http://techcrunch.com/tag/baidu.

8. Tencent Company fact sheet, www.tencent.com/en-us/at/abouttencent.shtml.

9. Paul Mozur, "What China Can Teach Facebook," *Wall Street Journal,* May 18, 2012, http://blogs.wsj.com.

10. Data access through yahoo finance on March 9, 2013, http://finance.yahoo.com/q/ks?s=0700.HK+Key+Statistics.

11. Walters et al., "The World's Next E-Commerce Superpower."

12. Li & Fung Research Centre, "China's Online Retailing Market, 2011," October 2011, www.funggroup.com/eng/knowledge/research/china_dis_issue90.pdf.

13. "E-Commerce in China: The Great Leap Online," *Economist*, November 26, 2011.

14. "China E-Commerce," January 2012, www.slideshare.net/thempro/china-ecommerce-2011.

15. Ibid.

16. Simon Kemp, "Social, Digital, and Mobile in China," *We Are Social*, January 23, 2013, wearesocial.net/blog/2013/01/social-digital-mobile-china-2.

17. "China E-Commerce."

18. Li & Fung, "China's Online Retailing Market, 2011."

19. Ibid.; and Walters et al., "The World's Next E-Commerce Superpower."

20. "Social, Digital, and Mobile in China."

21. Walters et al., "The World's Next E-Commerce Superpower."

22. "Social, Digital, and Mobile in China."

23. "Evolution of Brand: China Social Media Campaigns," *Little Red Book*, July 14, 2010, www.littleredbook.com.

24. Han Han, *Han Han Digest*, www.hanhandigest.com.

25. Michael Zung, "Digital Luxury in China: Case Studies Show It's Not Too Late to Start!", June 9, 2011, Clickz.asia, www.clickz.asia/3576/3576.

CHAPTER 7

Distribution Issues and Trends

In the fall of 2010, the British grocery giant Tesco started thinking about how to gain market share for its chain of Home Plus supermarkets in South Korea. The company explored how it might be able to gain access to new consumers and increase its market share without the necessity of large capital outlays to build new stores. It was a daunting challenge and required new thinking. The new ideas generated by the company produced an innovative way to reach consumers that is rapidly making its way around the world.

Instead of building new stores, Tesco set up what has become known as a *virtual store* in the country's subway stations. Riding the subway can sometimes be monotonous, especially for those who take the same route back and forth every morning and evening to and from their jobs. Commuting along the same daily path can lead to the endless task of figuring out how to keep the mind engaged. Reading a newspaper, working on a crossword puzzle, or reading a book are some of the most commonly chosen activities.

The pervasive rise of the smartphone has made time consumption a lot easier on these kinds of commutes, and it is the smart phone that Tesco began centering on in its new strategy on to reach new customers in new ways. Mobile phones are ubiquitous in South Korea. The country has one of the highest mobile penetration rates in the world and a user base that consumes data services ferociously.

Tesco used these insights and found a place where lost time and unused space could be put to work. Standing on numerous subway platforms in the city of Seoul, consumers now can see and browse brightly lit pictures of grocery store shelves full of staple goods. This is the virtual store. Located on the subway platform and hung between the subway car doors, these brightly lit pictures look almost identical to a grocery shelf. Instead of commuters looking at their watches, they now shop for groceries.

Consumers download a smartphone application that enables them to use the mobile phone's camera to scan the product bar code on an item and place an order. For morning commuters, the products they ordered while standing on the platform will most likely be waiting for them when they arrive home in the evening. "Attention, commuters, the nightly milk run on the way home from work has now been automated." With this new solution in place, Tesco's online orders are shooting through the roof, and the sought-after market share gains are being achieved.

Less than a year later, the concept is being imported to China and coming to the subway stations of Shanghai. Yihaodian, one of the leading grocery e-commerce companies in China, has deployed the same kind of virtual stores at nine metro lines in the Shanghai subway system. The company has a long history with Walmart, which last year announced it was taking a larger, ownership equity stake in the firm. Bringing virtual storefronts to Shanghai's subway system is one of Yihaodian's new market initiatives launched since Walmart's announcement.

"The virtual supermarket targets young, tech-savvy consumers who don't have time to shop the conventional way," a Yihaodian representative explained.[1] "The idea is to bring convenience to busy people, who can buy what they need and want during their daily commute." The number of daily commuters in Shanghai is soon set to reach 9 million. And they are busy people, driven by frenetic working lives. Now the grocery store is coming to them, reaching these consumers at a new point of purchase.

Virtual stores are just one of the innovations combining e-commerce and distribution that are reaching more consumers in China. These cutting-edge innovations exist alongside the more traditional practices of the developing economy and its historical state-run legacy. Some things seem backward—regressive, even. Yet the future is here, too.

This is especially true as the market moves inland, where the modern physical infrastructure has just come into place in the last 10 years and a thriving consumer digital landscape (described in Chapter 6) has developed. In these inland markets, rising affluence is creating a new consumer-driven economy. The demand is there and rising. The question is whether the existing distribution infrastructure for consumer goods is evolving rapidly enough to keep pace.

Overview of the Distribution Structure

Before China's modern economy emerged, the country's distribution infrastructure was locally based, fragmented, and push-driven, with goods moving through the distribution chain irrespective of real consumer demand. A distribution chain that is *pull driven* uses endpoint consumer demand to determine how many goods are driven through the system and where they go. A *push-driven* system uses the opposite approach, assessing how many goods can be made and then allocating them across the distribution chain by other means. In the previous age of product scarcity, meeting demand with the drab products produced by a state-run economy was not a driving principle. With too few staple goods to meet full demand, political considerations and product rationalization were the two issues overriding the existing distribution system. These decisions around product allocation and who received what goods were made by a centralized bureaucracy. With a lack of hard infrastructure, goods moved slowly and passed through multiple middlemen before reaching the few points of retail that existed in end markets. Reaching the end of the chain meant that the goods arrived at the one or two mom-and-pop retail stores in small towns and rural areas.

Lack of consumer choice, multiple levels of distributors, and product supply separated from any notion of demand were the system's core characteristics. As Figure 7.1 illustrates, today's distribution system has become a hybrid of a more efficient system and the multiple-level system of the past. China's distribution system, like other points across the value chain, is very fragmented. There are thousands of distribution companies competing intensely for business.

Over the course of several generations, these domestic distributors have continued to evolve and become a market force. They have tightly entwined connections with provincial governments. This evolution has mirrored the growth of legacy department store companies, which are also largely

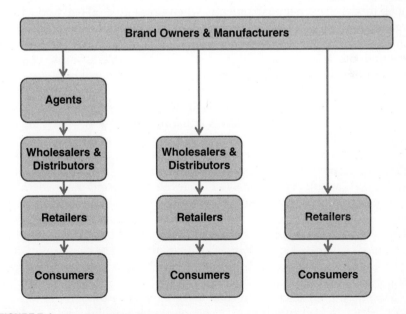

FIGURE 7.1 China's Distribution System

entrenched in individual provinces and supported by local governments. As such, domestic distributors have a great expertise in navigating the complex and often ambiguous world of business relationships.

Largely confined to a regional breadth of coverage, domestic distributors have developed strong networks over generations that can often reach the most far-flung village. Most of these players do not offer much capability beyond the loading, shipping, and delivery services, though. Quality is not necessarily the foremost concern, either. For example, almost every expressway in China is governed by a toll system, which raises the cost of logistics on a per-truck basis.

The market's response to this situation has been to overload trucks. Any car ride on a local expressway in China provides a view of shipping trucks loaded significantly over the point of full capacity and beyond the threshold of safety and product quality. As these overloaded trucks shift from lane to lane, the goods sway from side to side. One hopes that the ropes around the shipping containers stacked above and beyond the truck's walls will hold, preventing a terrible accident. Often, the ropes do not hold the containers, and traffic is halted for hours.

The core assets of domestic distributors are deep relationships, knowledge of local markets, and consumer reach. Because of a lack of more sophisticated capabilities, these companies compete primarily in price, raising the level of cutthroat competition.

As modern retail has expanded into inland markets, more efficient distribution models have begun to emerge. When China entered the World Trade Organization (WTO) in 2001, it precipitated the entry of foreign distribution companies to the market three years later. In accordance with China's membership in the WTO, these foreign distributors were able to secure country-wide distribution licenses, and many moved toward national coverage.

These companies have imported more sophisticated capabilities into the market, such as product tracking, marketing expertise, and other value-added services. These relatively new players in the market are less willing to compete in price. Old and new structures collaborate, with foreign-based distributors increasingly acting as the first point of contact to modern retail customers and then partnering with domestic-based distributors for greater access within local markets and to supply the more fragmented mom-and-pop outlets.[2]

The entry and development of foreign-owned distributors has in many ways mirrored the entry and development of the modern foreign-owned retailers in the market. Both have wider geographical operations and bring more modern management capability than their domestic counterparts. Table 7.1 outlines the key differences between domestic and foreign-owned distributors.

Despite the advances in recent years, China's distribution infrastructure is characterized by multiple levels of wholesalers, agents, and other middlemen, each without much investment in information technology or

TABLE 7.1 Key Differences between Domestic and Foreign-Owned Distributors

Domestic Distributors	Foreign-Owned Distributors
Development in the era of a state-controlled economy and product scarcity.	Broader geographical reach.
	Greater emphasis on value-added capabilities.
Basic level of distribution services.	
Local concentration, with deep reach into respective markets.	Less depth in local markets.
	Less competition in price.
Multigenerational relationships with retailers and local governments.	

sophisticated capabilities to serve their customers. This environment creates the following challenges for future improvements and efficiencies:

- Far removed from the end distribution point, brand manufacturers struggle with influencing their presence at the shelf. This has broad implications for shelf presentation.
- Price management across regions is extremely difficult. Lack of visibility to retail price is the first reason. The second reason is tracing price discrepancies back to the source distributors. The third reason is that the local fragmentation of the distributor base creates greater opportunities for diversion and arbitrage.
- Marketing investments made at retail are almost impossible to validate and measure.

With so many changing hands in the distribution chain, companies' chief incentives move away from delivering to customers and meeting demand and toward maximizing their profitability in their small slice of the chain. While the market is moving to rationalize the number of middlemen in the chain, a residue of arms-length relationships exist, with a subtle adversarial nature remaining in the market. This legacy manifests itself in reportedly toxic relationships between retailers and manufacturers.

Distributors, agents, wholesalers, and third-party logistics companies make up a logistics network that currently centers on the following three primary areas in the market:

1. **The Bohai Rim.** This includes the markets in the northeastern provinces north of the capital city, Beijing.
2. **The Yangtze River Delta.** This includes the markets from the southeastern coastal provinces to the inland eastern provinces that follow the Yangtze River.
3. **The Pearl River Delta.** The most inland of the three centers, this includes the areas around Chongqing and Chengdu.

These areas of distribution are highlighted in Figure 7.2.[3]

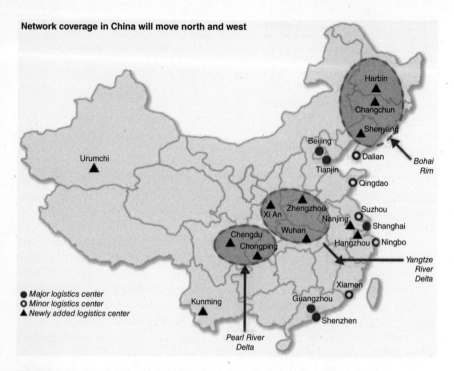

FIGURE 7.2 China's Distribution Hubs

Source: A. T. Kearney, *China 2015: Transportation and Logistics Strategies,* 2010, www
.atkearney.com/paper/-/asset_publisher/dVxv4Hz2h8bS/content/china-2015-transportation-
and-logistics-strategies/10192

These central points of distribution can be paired with the demand
cluster and market segmentation analysis presented in Chapter 4. This analysis, based on consumer economic indicators, grouped areas of consumer
demand in the Chinese market at the provincial level into geographical
clusters.

The mapping of the distribution hubs to the consumer demand clusters
provides a view of how supply chain networks might evolve in the market to reach and serve more consumers. Industry data suggest that these
geographical centers of distribution are changing. The Pearl River Delta is
developing as economic growth increases along with foreign direct investment. More investment in warehousing is moving south from Shanghai. This
implies that the current distribution area of the Yangtze River Delta may
split into two areas: one serving the southern coastal areas aligned with the
provinces in the Guangdong demand cluster, and one serving the provinces
that go inland along the Yangtze River, included in the Anhui demand cluster (see Table 7.2).

TABLE 7.2 Relation of Demand Clusters to Distribution Centers

Demand Cluster	Included Provinces	Nearest Distribution Hub
Guangdong	• Guangdong • Fujian • Guangxi • Hainan • Jiangxi • Shanghai • Zhejiang	Yangtze River Delta
Beijing	• Beijing • Heilongjiang • Hebei • Inner Mongolia • Jilin • Liaoning • Shandong • Shanxi • Tianjin	Bohai Rim
Anhui	• Anhui • Henan • Hubei • Hunan • Jiangsu	Yangtze River Delta
Chengdu	• Sichuan • Chongqing • Gansu • Guizhou • Ningxia • Qinghai • Shaanxi • Xingjiang • Tibet • Yunnan	Pearl River Delta

The geographical distribution hubs are showing infrastructure development and investment aligned with the consumption indicators of the market.

Closing the Consumer Trust Gap

Consumer trust has become the driving force for distribution advancements in China. Yes, trust. It's not usually the first thing that comes to mind when most people think about the impetus for improving distribution. Usually, cost and margin expansion lead the way almost exclusively. In the race toward earnings targets and competitive success, distribution and cost reduction seem inevitably linked and are on equal footing, but this is not the case in China. A survey conducted by IBM's Institute of Business Value found that profitability is high on the list of supply chain executives but that other considerations are being given higher priority relative to other, more mature economies. The survey consolidated responses from more than 600 supply chain executives in China and compared those answers to the results of similar surveys in other countries.[4]

Figure 7.3 highlights the differences in distribution and supply chain priorities between China and the mature economies of Japan, the United States, and Western Europe. The chart is a summary of the survey respondents' replies when they were asked to rank their top supply chain and distribution priorities. Note that profitability, cost, and responsiveness were significantly higher for the mature economies and far less important in China's market. The one category ranked higher by China-based executives was product quality, and it represented the largest difference in all categories. The respondents from China ranked product quality 22 percent higher in importance than the respondents based in the mature economies.

China's business executives clearly believe that product quality carries unique importance in their market. This may come as a surprise. Given the market's relative lack of sophistication and the presence of more middlemen, inventory levels must be excessive, compared to more mature markets. The opportunity to reduce costs and increase responsiveness must be enormous. Why the significantly higher focus on product quality, then? The answer is lack of trust among consumers for product quality. In recent years,

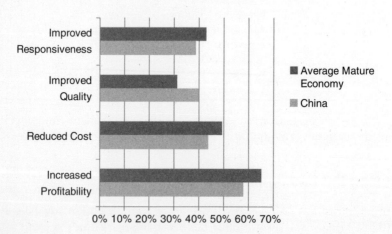

FIGURE 7.3 China's Distribution and Supply Chain Priorities Compared to Those of Mature Economies

that lack of trust has led not only to disappointed consumers but also to consumers frightened for their safety.

China's Food-Safety Crisis

China's consumers are a scared lot. Since 2008, when the poisonous chemical melamine was found in infant formula and directly blamed for the deaths of 6 children and the nonfatal poisoning of 300 more, China has endured one food poisoning scandal after another. It seems that a food scandal is discovered every week and is a regular part of the news cycle and Internet chatter.

Here are some examples of the food scandals written about recently in the Chinese media:

- Restaurants using "recycled" cooking oil reclaimed from sewers, containing known carcinogens.
- Dairy products recalled after melamine was discovered through product sample testing.
- Pork relabeled and sold as beef after the chemical borax was added. Borax is an acidic cleaning agent commonly found in laundry detergents and household cleaners.
- Consumers reporting that pork they had purchased was laced with bacteria and glowed in the dark.
- Hundreds of people falling ill after eating pork laced with ractopamine. This additive spurs leaner muscle growth when consumed by pigs, but it causes nausea when consumed by people.[5]
- Noodle manufacturers caught adding ink and paraffin wax to give their products the look and texture of more expensive noodles.
- Aquatic farmers feeding ground-up birth control pills to some breeds of fish to make them mature faster. Birth control pills cost virtually nothing because of China's strict limits on family size and the government's family planning policy.[6]

Government inspectors have even found that in some cases, eggs are not really eggs. Instead, using instructions available on the Internet, someone has created an egglike concoction from gelatin and oleate, which is used to make soap, and these fake eggs have found their way into the food chain.[7]

These are just a few of the recent, more widely reported food scandals in China. "These publicized food safety scandals represent only a fraction of unsafe food production practices," reported *Caixin*, a leading magazine in China. "Hundreds of chemical food additives are pumped into products that Chinese people consume every day."[8]

Modern retailers and brand manufacturers have not been unscathed by these scandals. Walmart was forced to close a number of stores in Chongqing after it was discovered that the pork sold at these sites was mislabeled.[9] The Coca-Cola Company temporarily shut down a production facility after rumors circulated of chlorine being found in its soda.[10] Many more foreign companies have experienced problems with product quality and, facing intense scrutiny, may suffer from more consumer backlash in such scandals.

Although there has been much public attention on this issue since the melamine tragedy, and many promises have been made to correct the problems, food scandals have only seemed to escalate. Perhaps incidents of food poisoning are reported more widely than they used to be. Certainly the Chinese government is encouraging the media to expose those who intentionally contaminate food bound for the open market. The media are often used in tandem with government crackdowns to resolve these kinds of issues.

But in the last few years the government's hand has proved largely ineffective in rooting out the sources of contamination. The Chinese government's ability to better enforce food safety laws appears in question. One of the major reasons for continued food scandals is the immensity of the challenge in policing the system. There are 166 million farms operating across the country, many composed of individual plots. The fragmentation continues further up the value chain, with simply too many food companies to monitor. With greater media attention, consumer concern and anxiety about food safety have only heightened.

Thank goodness there is an app for that. Government's inability to ensure a safe food supply has created an opportunity for app builders on the ubiquitous iPhone. In the spring of 2012, a new iPhone app was released that aggregates and reports all news related to food scandals and thus helps users to avoid tainted food.[11] The app's popularity indicates the widespread concern about these issues.

Consumers are starting to take other steps as well to protect themselves from a food system that is increasingly viewed as unsafe. Well-to-do professionals have been known to travel abroad to purchase food for their children. In some cases, albeit on the fringe today, consumers are beginning to simply eliminate meat from their diets. In the span of just a few years, troves of vegetarian restaurants have opened in the capital city of Beijing. Concern for personal safety, rather than normal health concerns or a philosophy about ecology and/or animals, is believed to be at the root of these dietary conversions.[12]

Food safety, and the accompanying consumer anxiety, has reached crisis proportions in China. An emphasis on the necessity of a more tightly controlled distribution chain has therefore increased in importance, rising above all other factors.

Counterfeit Products

Another key issue creating a lack of consumer trust is the widespread presence of counterfeit goods. Counterfeit consumer products represent a $20 billion annual problem in terms of lost revenue for branded manufacturers. Some estimates suggest that as much as 70 percent of the goods sold on the market in China today are fake.[13]

In previous years, counterfeit products were largely separate from the branded value chain. Consumers who sought counterfeit merchandise—and there were many—went to large well-known markets to purchase faux-branded merchandise. In these markets, every kind of fake product was—and still is, for that matter—available for purchase. Hermes, Prada, Nike, and every other well-known brand is represented. People knew what they were purchasing and did so with gusto.

Over time, though, counterfeit merchandise has found its way into more established distribution chains. This is happening just as the consumers who once gravitated to counterfeit markets are losing their taste for fake goods. In a recent survey, consumers reported that they are less willing to buy counterfeit goods—a decrease from 30 percent to just above 10 percent in the span of four years.

Now there is rising doubt among consumers who are seeking genuine branded merchandise on whether they are purchasing the genuine article. In 2009, estimates indicated that more than 30 percent of mobile phones in the market were *shangzhai*, or clever fakes.[14] A well-publicized case in 2011 discovered counterfeit goods in a well-known, upscale furniture chain catering to wealthy Chinese. The company's suppliers, Italian-based leather and furniture manufacturers, faced a backlash online as consumers vented their outrage. Legal action followed. This is an example of how retailers that marketed themselves as havens from counterfeits are increasingly falling victim to their pervasive spread.[15]

For years, the threat of counterfeits acted as a barrier to the growth of e-commerce. Consumers were concerned that after they purchased genuine branded items on a web site, the products would be switched for fraudulent goods during the delivery process. Alibaba, whose Taobao site is the e-commerce leader, introduced a new innovation named Alipay, China's answer to PayPal, which comes with a distinctive Chinese flavor rooted in solving consumers' skepticism.

Unlike PayPal, which executes a payment transaction at the time of purchase, Alipay defers the payment transaction until the goods have been received. This allows for consumer inspection and validation of the order. This small change resulted in Alipay reaching a commanding leadership position in online transaction management, and it helped to solve the consumer trust gap related to counterfeit goods. Taobao has pledged a renewed effort in recent years to combat and rid its online marketplace of counterfeit goods. Yet many branded manufacturers, especially in the luxury market, remain unconvinced and are opting to control their distribution chain through ownership of their own retail and online stores rather than facing the risks otherwise.

The pervasive problem of food safety and counterfeit goods creates a lack of trust between the manufacturers and retailers and the consumers they serve. Food safety in particular appears to be a problem that is getting worse, not better. Branded companies, retailers, and the government clearly recognize improvement as a top priority, and the resolution of these problems lie at the heart of any actions to improve the distribution chain.

Distribution Trends

Distribution trends in the Chinese market for consumer goods are directed toward closing the consumer trust gap.

Cold Chain Distribution

One of the largest challenges in ensuring a quality, consistent product is the absence of cold chain logistics in China. In developed markets, a mature cold chain ensures that perishable products are transported at a consistent temperature from manufacturer to shelf. An effective cold chain is characterized by consistent temperature control during transportation, effective control and equipment for storage, and efficient cycle times and standardized processes for managing the transition points in the logistics chain, such as cross-docking. With these capabilities in place, consumers can expect products purchased at shelf to be free of heat-related bacteria, fresh, and ready to be safely consumed. Products such as fruit and vegetables will not be rotten. Ice cream bars will be neither melted nor rock-hard frozen.

The capabilities that make up an effective cold chain are largely absent in today's logistics chain in China. A study by the consultancy A. T. Kearney estimates that China has just two refrigerated trucks for every 10,000 middle-class consumers, compared to nine in the United States. The gap in cold storage is even wider, with 1.6 cubic feet in China per middle-class consumer, compared to 13 cubic feet in the United States.

In addition to the lack of temperature-controlled assets, the number of middlemen in the logistics chain also increases the risk of spoilage. Thus there is a substantial risk to quality, brand erosion, and the health of the

Chinese consumer.[16] The following facts about the current situation of China's cold chain distribution show the challenges that lie ahead:

- As much as 35 percent of fresh food rots in the distribution chain.
- An estimated 10 to 15 percent of meat spoils, compared to less than 3 percent in mature markets.
- Only 15 percent of fresh food is transported in refrigerated trucks, compared to approximately 90 percent in mature markets.

A breakdown at any point in the distribution chain is a point of failure, defined as a product with a temperature outside the desired range. An example of a breakdown in a cold chain is an excessive unloading time of more than one hour. Even when the products are transported in refrigerated trucks, the lack of cold storage at a warehouse is another point of failure. More than 80 percent of food loss in China's distribution chain is caused by a lack of adequate transportation and excessive loading and unloading times.[17]

Meeting these challenges is often delegated to the suppliers, who have borne the majority of the costs in improving cold chain issues. However, retailers are beginning to see the cost and sales benefits of improving perishable distribution from their distribution centers to the stores. The involvement of third-party distributors in the past few years came with the promise of an improved cold storage infrastructure. Yet, industry-wide trials have been slow to generate infrastructure growth in this area, and large brand manufacturers such as Procter & Gamble build and operate their own cold chain network. Like other areas of distribution, leading manufacturers have pioneered advancements largely through their own experimentation, embracing a do-it-yourself ethos that has led to a wide variety of distribution approaches and models (see "Do-It-Yourself Distribution" sidebar).

Direct Purchasing

Another trend leading to greater distribution efficiency and control is the substantial increase in direct purchasing between retailers and manufacturers. Historically, effective management and control of the distribution chain has been extremely difficult because of the lack of visibility and accountability resulting from the involvement of so many middlemen. For branded goods, a direct purchasing interface between the retailer chain and the brand manufacturer is increasingly becoming the norm. According to a recent survey, 89 percent of Chinese-based chain retailers are increasing the number of goods they purchase directly. Product safety was cited by a majority of those surveyed as a key driver in this move.

Centralized purchasing is a related trend. The ambitious plans initially announced by retailers have been tempered somewhat, indicating that the early moves to centralization were a bit too aggressive. Yet indications are that retail buying organizations have been restructured and that early experiments have enabled retailers to fine-tune their approach. The process and infrastructure to facilitate more direct buying from suppliers is now in place, is set to increase significantly, and is fast becoming a standard practice.

The flip side of the direct purchasing relationship with large branded manufacturers is the direct purchasing initiatives established between retailers and farms. Retailers have been moving aggressively the past five years to establish direct sources of supply with Chinese farmers. Carrefour's farm-to-fork initiative was announced in 2007 and has since grown to encompass a majority of the chain's perishable food products.[18] Walmart's initiative encompasses at least 36 established sourcing bases in different regions in China and oversees buying relationships with approximately 400,000 farmers. These efforts were initiated in 2008 by the Chinese government, which views these efforts as instrumental in making strides in product safety.

Direct Farm Sourcing

Equally important in the eyes of the government is direct farm sourcing, which passes cost savings on to the consumers through direct purchasing. Carrefour reports that direct farm sourcing allows products to be priced 15 to 20 percent cheaper than they would be otherwise. As a result of the government program, retailers' purchasing contracts also ensure guaranteed pricing to farmers. These factors act as downward pressure on the continued problem of inflationary food prices. Food inflation is an area of large sensitivity to the Chinese government, which fears that increasing food prices could lead to heightened social unrest.

Product Tracking

Some manufacturers, such as the pharmaceutical firm GlaxoSmithKline, are also investing in product tracking and tracing capability in order to prevent counterfeiting and the sales of out-of-date products.[19] Drug companies have been leading in this area because of the high dollar value per unit of their products and the inherent liability involved when fraudulent products are consumed.

The Results of These Trends

These distribution channel improvements will help to close the consumer trust gap. More direct procurement by retailers will mean greater visibility and accountability to organizations and people in the steps leading to the retail shelf. Fewer intermediaries in the channel will mean lower costs, which can be passed on to the consumers. A more effective cold chain will raise consumer confidence that the products they purchase and eat are fresh and safe. Progress is being made, but it will take time.

These distribution trends do not necessarily bode well for the domestic distributor of old, however. Old state-run monopolies, enforced by regional borders and ties to provincial governments, are giving way to new market structures. Foreign-owned distributors with greater capability and national scope will intensify the level of competition. Domestic distributors' value proposition are likely to evolve on a short-term basis. Some will expand their levels of coverage and capability to compete in that arena with the new market entrants.

The path for most will be to rely on their legacy advantages of deep local coverage and ties to local governments. They will probably partner with national distributors to fill in the gaps in market coverage. Not all will survive. For branded manufacturers looking to maximize consumer reach, the market realities and current direction suggest multiple routes to market based on targeted consumer segments, breadth of geographical reach, and depth of market penetration in local markets.

Do-it-Yourself Distribution: Companies Are Succeeding in Building Their Own

Without much in the way of established precedent and leading practices—and with an urgency to tap the market—companies are creating their own distribution strategies and networks from scratch. As a result, many structures and strategies are being implemented that act as a source of experimentation, a sort of "distribution school" that others can learn from. The following is a list of what some of the leading companies are doing in the area of distribution:

- Walmart has chosen a centralized strategy. The company is currently operating three distribution centers in China, each serving approximately 100 stores. This concentrated set of distribution centers facilitates Walmart's intent to move more goods to centralized purchasing centers and reach greater economies of scale. Approximately 85 percent of the goods move through this network, which can reach each of its stores within a day. Merchandising and assortments in the market remain local. Consumers' preference and climate differ drastically by region, which the company will need to accommodate to within this centralized model.

Continued

- Carrefour has chosen a decentralized model for its distribution network. The company operates more than 20 separate but small distribution centers across the country. Purchasing and distribution management and organizations are therefore much more localized.
- Yum! Brands, the company behind Pizza Hut, Kentucky Fried Chicken, and Taco Bell, is a well-known success story in China. Its distribution strategy is focused on control, consistency, and quality. The company operates 18 distribution centers in China. Although it doesn't own the real estate, the company focuses on owning the human capital and process to execute distribution. It uses its own truck fleet to service top-tier cities and outsourced trucking companies to fill in the market gaps, servicing more than 4,500 restaurants in more than 800 cities. The company oversees its inbound suppliers of poultry, which are geographically concentrated in a few provinces. This involves rail and barge transportation in the company's distribution network.

As more capability evolves in the market, standards in distribution networks and practices are coming to the fore. They will coexist with the do-it-yourself model of consumer goods distribution put in the place by the market pioneers. Their differences and their strategic emphases offer lessons to companies looking to further optimize their networks.

Source: Yum! Brands, David F. Miller Center for Retailing Education and Research

Retailer-Supplier Partnerships

More and more branded suppliers of consumer goods are engaging in direct relationships with retailers. As the retailing market has consolidated in the mature markets of Western Europe and North America, many of these suppliers have invested heavily in dedicated teams to serve the large retailers. These teams provide highly specialized capabilities in shopper segmentation, promotion management, and replenishment tailored to the needs of each specific retailer.

As the downstream markets have consolidated, more resources have been allocated to raise the level of service to a smaller number of large retailers. These teams collaborate with the teams from their retail customers on joint initiatives that span the spectrum of their joint operations. In other words, these companies have become quite good at managing and working with large retailers. That level of sophistication might lead many to think that these capabilities could be transferred to highly productive collaborative relationships with retailers in the Chinese market.

But that kind of structure and relationship has yet to find a home in China. Perhaps because of the legacy of a push distribution system with multiple organizations to haggle with, retailer and supplier relationships are reported to be dismal. The state of these relationships becomes the third pillar, after food safety and counterfeiting, in the consumer trust gap. The many issues that contribute to an adversarial relationship include the following:

- **Retailer slotting fees.** Retailers' charged fees are viewed as both ambiguous and onerous. It can cost a branded manufacturer millions of dollars in transaction fees just to establish a shelf presence in a few markets inside the country. Typically, most retailers, including foreign-based retailers that do not engage to the same usage level of fee structures elsewhere, also engage in the practice. Legal guidelines, vague and variable by region, add to the frustration and confusion. "Entrance fees and promotion expenses legitimate in some cities are considered bribery in others," according to a report by the Li & Fung Research Centre.[20] National laws passed in the last few years are intended to bring more consistency to these fees.
- **Information exchange.** Very few chain retailers are actively sharing point-of-sale and other operational data with suppliers. This practice has very much become the norm in more mature markets and has enabled significant advances in operational efficiency, promotional effectiveness, and other demand-creating programs. When branded companies are more vertically integrated and operate their own retail channels, primarily in the luxury goods market, the data are mined and used extensively.
- **Payment terms.** Retailers routinely use long payment terms to fund their working capital needs. More than a quarter of retailers in China engage in payment terms of more than 45 days. Recent government laws are designed to limit payment terms and resolve what many view as an unfair usage of commercial purchasing activities.

In the fall of 2010, a rift between Kraft Foods, the global consumer goods powerhouse, and Lianhua, China's largest grocer, went public and highlighted the tense relationship between these two giants in the consumer value chain.[21] Although it is unclear exactly what transpired, reports suggest that Kraft was unwilling to accept Lianhua's terms for additional discounts for its products. Despite that fact that Kraft held a commanding share in the market, Lianhua believed it could effectively push for substantial discounts. Instead, Kraft dug in its heels, an impasse developed, and Kraft's products were pulled from the shelves for a few months.

Although it appears that these issues were resolved in early 2011, they highlight the lack of trust involved in many retailer-supplier relationships, and they may also have motivated government action to clarify guidelines for commercial relationships between the two parties. Along with food safety issues and counterfeit products, the lack of trust between consumer-products companies and retailers acts as a barrier toward further improvement in the delivery of value to consumers.

Today's distribution network in China is focused on initiatives and capabilities to close these gaps with consumers. Closing these gaps is fundamental to improving consumers' expectations for safe food and genuine products. To do so, retailers are developing capabilities to deliver perishable items with consistent quality and establishing direct sourcing to manufacturers and farms. Better and more collaborative relationships between retailers and suppliers will facilitate these initiatives and help to close this gap faster (see Figure 7.4).

Today's supply chain and distribution infrastructure in China has grown significantly in its level of sophistication. A growing focus by large retail chains, multinational consumer products companies, and more sophisticated third-party logistics companies have raised the performance bar. Yet much remains to be done. China's continued food scandals highlight the supply chain's inability to deliver safe foods at a level of product quality that consumers expect. The proliferation of counterfeit goods has found its way into established distribution channels and threatens brand manufacturers' credibility with consumers. Relationships between retailers and suppliers are often strained.

Since its early days, modern retail has offered the promise of solving these issues and closing the gap in consumer trust. In the view of the average Chinese consumer, the nearest hypermarket is the safe, convenient alternative to the outside "wet" market. That expectation will be upheld as more consistency, control, and accountability are created in the distribution chain.

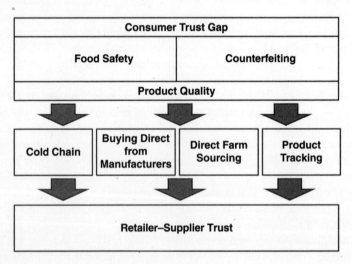

FIGURE 7.4 Closing the Gap in Consumer Trust

Notes

1. Jane Leung, "Shanghai Follows Seoul Down to the Virtual Subway Supermarket," CNN International, August 4, 2011, http://travel.cnn.com/shanghai/life/virtual-supermarket-hits-shanghai-subway-702139.

2. Li & Fung Research Centre, "Selling to the Source: A Closer Look into Wholesale Distribution Landscape in China," *China Distribution & Trading*, Issue 62, October 2009, www.funggroup.com/eng/knowledge/research/china_dis_issue62.pdf.

3. A. T. Kearney, *China 2015: Transportation and Logistics Strategies*, 2010, www.atkearney.com/paper/-/asset_publisher/dVxv4Hz2h8bS/content/china-2015-transportation-and-logistics-strategies/10192.

4. Heino Huettner and Winnie Song, "Follow the Leaders: Scoring High on the Supply Chain Maturity Model—Mainland China Perspectives on Supply Chain Fulfillment," IBM Global Business Services, IBM Institute for Business Value, 2007, www-935.ibm.com/services/us/gbs/bus/pdf/g510-6633-00-follow-leader-china-ff.pdf.

5. Laurie Burkitt, "Watermelon Scandal Bursts in China," *Wall Street Journal*, May 17, 2011.

6. Barbara Demick, "China Wrestles with Food Safety Problems." *Los Angeles Times,* June 26, 2011.

7. Sharon LaFraniere, "In China, Fear of Fake Eggs and 'Recycled' Buns," *New York Times,* May 7, 2011.

8. Quoted in Mark McDonald, "From Milk to Peas, a Chinese Food-Safety Mess," *International Herald Tribune*, June 21, 2012.

9. "In the Gutter," *Economist*, October 29, 2011.

10. "China Shuts Coke Plant after Chlorine Reports," Mother Nature Network, April 30, 2012, www.mnn.com.

11. McDonald, "From Milk to Peas."

12. Craig Nelson, "After Food Scandals, Growing Number of Chinese Reject Meat for Vegetarianism," *National*, May 31, 2011.

13. Mark Litke, "China Big in Counterfeit Goods," ABC News, April 21, 2012, www.abcnews.com.

14. "Pro Logo Chinese Consumers Are Falling Out of Love with Fakes," *Economist,* January 14, 2012.

15. David Barboza, "Chinese Upset over Counterfeit Furniture," *New York Times,* July 18, 2011.

16. Jim Morehouse and Mike Moriarty, "Food Safety in China: What It Means for Global Companies," AT Kearney, December 2007, http://newsletter.coldstoredesign.com/December07/Foodsafetyinchina.pdf.

17. David F. Miller, "Retail Supply Management Chain," Center for Retailing Education and Research, https://site.warrington.ufl.edu/iret/modules-on-retailing-in-china/module-6-retail-supply-chain-management.

18. Cao Zhen, "Carrefour Shenzhen Expands 'Farm-to-Fork' Program," *Shenzhen Daily*, April 14, 2011.

19. "Pro Logo Chinese Consumers."

20. *Distribution in China*, Li & Fung Research Centre, Fung Group, September 2012, page 8, www.funggroup.com/eng/knowledge/research/china_dis_issue101.pdf.

21. Since this event occurred, Kraft has split into two separate companies, Kraft Foods and Mondelez International. I have chosen to use a designation consistent with the timing of that event.

CHAPTER 8

Hefei: Home of the World's Next-Generation Consumer

The Chinese consumer growth story is beginning to happen in places unfamiliar to many. The highest economic growth rates are happening outside the commercial and government capitals inland. The city that best profiles these on ramps to China's new consumer economy is Hefei. This city's characteristics and growing importance are examined in this chapter. In order to give the reader a better understanding of the significance of this Hefei, let us first take a look at its official sister city in the United States—Columbus, Ohio—as a means of comparison.

"As Ohio goes, so goes the nation" is an old, well-worn political maxim uttered every four years during the U.S. presidential election. Recent presidential elections have often been won by the slimmest of margins, with voters in Ohio casting the deciding votes. Because Ohio confers a large number of the electoral college votes required by those who hope to claim the prize, presidential candidates visit the state often and get to know its residents quite well. It is a hard-fought state, with residents whose opinions cross the U.S. political spectrum. Long a bastion of our nation's manufacturing economy, union organizers hit the streets hard for their candidates. Equal in number are those whose fervent views on policy align with those of other candidates. This political diversity causes clashes and competition in a region where every vote counts.

Life in the Middle

In the middle of the state lies the capital city of Columbus, which is located about 500 miles inland from New York City. Situated only 20 percent of the distance from the east to west coast, the city is considered squarely at the cultural center of what is known as Middle America. Columbus is a land-locked city lying north of the Ohio River, a major transportation waterway that leads to the Mississippi River, the fourth longest river in the world. Columbus also lies south of Lake Erie, one of the five Great Lakes, which contain approximately 20 percent of Earth's fresh water and have been integral to the economic development of the region.

Cincinnati, Ohio, approximately 100 miles southwest of Columbus, was founded on the Ohio River and thrived on its commercial uses. Cleveland, Ohio, approximately 130 miles north of Columbus, lies on Lake Erie, a location that defined the early economic progress that gave rise to the city.

Columbus, Cincinnati, and Cleveland are the three largest cities in Ohio. Whereas the founding and growth of Cincinnati and Cleveland were under-pinned by their proximity to water, the founding of the landlocked city of Columbus was fueled by political compromise. Two decades after Ohio had been formalized as a state, Ohio's politicians did not know where to locate their capital. No one was able to agree on the current site or on other cities that had previously played the role, so the governing politicians agreed to establish a new city as the state capital. And so Columbus was founded in 1816.

Today, Columbus is an economically diversified and vibrant city. The Ohio state government provides its own universe of services, legislators, and lobbyists, adding its contribution to an increasingly broad econom-ic spectrum. Many of the country's largest banks have big operations in Columbus, and large logistics companies have a presence at an intersection of the interstate highway system.

Columbus is also, to the surprise of many, a center of some of the lead-ing retail brands. In 1963, Les Wexner dropped out of law school to help out in his family's retail business. He borrowed $5,000 and built a multibil-lion dollar retail empire called Limited Brands. The company's most famous brand is Victoria's Secret, which entered the mass-market consciousness long ago. The company has spun off other leading brands, like Abercrom-bie & Fitch, which also has its corporate headquarters in Columbus.

Another force for economic diversification in the city is its numerous institutions of higher education, particularly Ohio State University, which make Columbus a college town. Ohio State University is reached by driving north from the city's center on High Street. For many people who experi-enced college education in the United States, driving up High Street past bar after bar sparks reminiscences of misspent nights in the college hangouts that help to define the American college experience. Just outside the univer-sity's main campus, High Street is the mecca of the Friday night social life for the more than 50,000 students attending the university.

The third largest university in the United States, Ohio State is a hav-en for students from across the Midwestern region of the United States and around the world.[1] Its sprawling campus is nearly 2,000 acres, and its campus buildings dot the landscape of the northern part of the city. With more than 40,000 employees, the university is a major driver of the local economy, generating more than $2 billion in economic impact each year.[2] The cutting-edge research of the medical school and other research institutions attracts a highly skilled labor pool to the city.

Ohio State also significantly influences the cultural life of Columbus. The "spiritual" end of High Street is Ohio Stadium, which is filled by more than 100,000 people who want to see their beloved football team, the Buckeyes, take to the field. On Saturdays during the college football season, the campus becomes the cultural center of the region. The games are always sold out. For those who are lucky enough to be season ticket holders, it is a common family tradition to pass them on from generation to generation. Following the Ohio State football team is a local religion for some fans.

The presence of the university, research institutions, hospitals, businesses, and a steady supply of educated labor all contribute to a durable, diversified local economy that has given Columbus more protection from economic hardships compared to other large cities in the region.

The economic heritage of the American Midwest includes heavy manufacturing. The steel and auto industries had built a large presence here in the past several generations. The decline of this manufacturing base in recent decades has led to an economic hollowing out across the region as low-skilled manufacturing jobs moved abroad. Unemployment has been rising and has yet to return to the lower levels seen during the heyday of the domestic auto industry. The northeastern portion of Ohio has yet to fully recover from the downturn in the steel industry more than 30 years ago. Continued economic decline has become a source of anxiety across the region. Yet the American dream survives at least a little more in Columbus.

The city is considered one of the best test markets in the country for new products. Its local population is considered representative of the larger United States. At the same time, the large student and international population at the university provides an opportunity to survey a wider demographic set of potential consumers. Economic diversity translates into a diverse population in terms of education, background, and community.

Advertising costs less in Columbus. While product success in Miami, Florida, does not forecast similar results in Butte, Montana, Columbus has proved to have the right mixture for a testing ground of future consumer success stories in the U.S. market. The headquarters of the fast-food chain Wendy's is located here, and the company often test-markets new ideas in its backyard.

"It has affordable media," a company spokesperson reported, "and you have the ability to advertise without messaging spilling over into adjacent markets. Columbus is also a younger town because of the university, and many OSU [Ohio State University] graduates stay in town [after graduating], meaning you have a vibrant 20- to 30-year-old population, and it's growing. Columbus is very representative of American demographics."[3]

Columbus is not, however, the first city to come up in the national conversation and does not reside at the forefront of the national consciousness. It's pretty safe to say that celebrities do not choose to live here. Though economically vibrant, it lacks the money culture of New York's Wall Street, London's traders, and Silicon Valley's venture capitalists. The city can be a little "off the radar."

There is no great classical novel set in Columbus that has helped to define the city as there has been for cities like New York. In *The Great Gatsby*, for instance, the main character, Nick Carraway, moves from the Midwest to New York, which is profiled by F. Scott Fitzgerald for its 1920s world of the rich, with clashes between old money and new. (Nevertheless, left morally bankrupt by his path, Nick does return to the Midwest—but that region is not the subject of the book.) *The Bonfire of the Vanities* by Tom Wolfe is another example of a book set in New York, this time in the financial market heyday of the 1980s. New York thus looms large in the nation's cultural identity in part because of a large body of literature that has used it as a backdrop.

If Columbus has any literary identity, it can be found in books by the once famous but now little-known journalist Bob Greene. Raised in a small town outside the city, Greene made his career in part through stories about the "way things used to be"—simple, sentimental stores about hardworking people and noble lives led honorably and largely anonymously.

In one of his most widely read books, *Be True to Your School*, Greene himself is the main character. Pulled from the pages of his high school diary, the story describes the trials and joys of adolescence in Columbus in a different, simpler time, 1964. The main character is sheltered and experiences the events of the time through television. It is a nostalgic story on the innocence of a child in a place apparently untouched by corruption.

People who live in Columbus tend to cite numerous benefits about the city. They love living in a university town that provides an influx of culture, youth, and sports. They cite the diversity of employers and good schools and the laid-back Midwestern vibe. Those characteristics contribute to an environment with a good quality of life, a manageable pace, and good prospects for the future.

China's Sibling

Half the world away in China, another capital city operates out of the cultural limelight of its country. Hefei is the capital city of its province, Anhui, and has much in common with its American sister city.

Hefei is located about 300 miles from China's commercial center, Shanghai. Although less than 20 percent of the distance from east to west, Hefei, like Columbus, is well inland (on the eastern edge of central China) and is considered far away from the commercial centers on the coast. Like Columbus, Hefei is landlocked. Far away from the Yangtze River, the commercial path to the south, Hefei has historically been isolated from the economic progress to the east.

The Yangtze River is the third largest river in the world, smaller only than the Nile and the Amazon, and it has served as the foundation for China's water transportation system. As a result, the cities on the banks of the Yangtze have historically benefited economically. During the export era of China's economic boom, more than 160 million rural migrants left their homes for the coastal economic zones to work in the factories, and Anhui was one of the major sources of this migration.

Also to the south of Hefei is the mountainous region of Huangshan, one of the most beautiful and photographed areas of China. The pictures of this region often have a mystical quality about them. If you have ever seen pictures from China of jagged mountains, interspersed with clouds and fog, they are likely from southern Anhui. To the north are the less visited arid plains and cities like Hefei. Like Columbus, Hefei was not the political capital of its region right away. Only in 1949 was it awarded that status.

Like Columbus, Hefei is a college town. Some of the country's leading institutions of higher learning are here. At least nine universities educate thousands of students in the city, creating a labor pool of educated workers and consumers. These universities support numerous scientific research centers, putting the city in a leadership position for the country in the number of research institutions.

Hefei has the same characteristics that make Columbus a test market for new retail and consumer goods products. Hefei's low cost keeps advertising spend down. Its lower retail presence requires less coordination and logistical support. Its population is both representative of the larger population and inclusive of the youthful diversity stemming from its universities. It is self-contained. Perhaps in the future we will read about Hefei as a test market for new products and services before a mainstream launch across the Chinese market.

Hefei's importance as a test market may already be coming to the forefront. At Stanford's China Internet Conference in 2011, Renren's CEO Joseph Chen highlighted the social media capabilities of its product through a case study of a retail market campaign conducted in Hefei. Describing Hefei as a college town, the CEO showed how his company created consumer demand and buzz for a retail client through a viral campaign, leading more consumers to their client's retail locations in the city. Hefei may even be moving into a position of helping to define the new products and services driving consumer engagement and economic growth.[4]

To the eyes of many, however, Hefei is considered an afterthought in discussions about China. Both the *Financial Times* and the *Guardian* recently described Hefei as a rural backwater, helping to cement the impression of the city as a faraway, unsophisticated, undeveloped city.[5] An author chronicling his travels across the country from east to west put it as follows: "You can be traveling across China, arrive in a city that is twice the size of Houston, and think, I've never even heard of this place. That is how it is for many foreign visitors to Hefei."[6]

Many Chinese have never been to Hefei and consider it to be a poor, agricultural region of the country. For those travelers, domestic and foreign, who travel farther inland, making it past the glitz of Shanghai and the temples of Beijing to arrive in Anhui province, the mountains to the south are favored over destinations to the north, where Hefei is located. Until the interstate highways and better rail service was established in recent years, Hefei was a pretty difficult place to get to. Despite being a few hundred miles from Shanghai, it could take hours through country roads or on slow trains to get there. People really had to go out of their way to get to Hefei, and few did.

The region's literary identity can be drawn from the classic novel *The Good Earth* by Pearl Buck. The Pulitzer Prize–winning novel is the story of a farmer in Anhui who struggles through lifelong poverty to finally achieve prosperity. His life consisted of having farmland, losing it, and then regaining ownership of it. Though set before the Second World War and the subsequent coming to power of the Communists, the story of economic struggle—centered on poverty, agriculture, and personal hardship—is a predominant lens that many use to view Anhui today.

Hefei Rises

The view of Hefei as a backwater is increasingly becoming obsolete. If Hefei is a backwater, it's a big one. Its metropolitan area sprawls across more than 2,700 square miles and has an approximate population of 5 million.[7] Its downtown area, surrounded by an ancient canal, continues to expand outward, swallowing up and transforming the countless nearby villages and towns that were once isolated and autonomous. The interstate system put in place in the last decade is changing those small villages into suburbs of the metroplex, reachable in minutes by car, whereas before it took hours to reach them traveling on dilapidated buses over dirt roads.

Hefei is experiencing a building boom. A subway is under construction. A new international airport opened in the spring of 2011 linking Hefei to the major domestic cities as well as to the commercial capitals throughout the region. The streets throughout the commercial center of the city are being widened to resolve traffic congestion. Quality of life is improving. Since 2005, the local government has made an effort to close down outdoor unregulated food markets believed to be unsanitary. These efforts have been part of a larger beautification project that is attempting to undo the industrial aura that fell over large parts of the city because of the push of the Communist Party in the 1950s to make the city an industrial center.

As labor costs rise in the competitive, mature markets on the coast, attention is moving inland for the next phase of growth in the consumer economy. Hefei has established itself as one of the next stops on that growth train and has become a thriving economic center. Multinational companies are recognizing these opportunities and moving in.

Chief among them is Unilever, which has migrated its entire Chinese manufacturing base to Hefei. In the late 2000s, Unilever started to foresee the changes happening in the Chinese market. With the majority of its manufacturing centers in Shanghai, the company became concerned about rising labor costs in its coastal operations. It also became increasingly focused on inland markets with higher growth potential.

In the last few years, the company has shifted seven factories from Shanghai to Hefei. The head of Unilever's business in north Asia said recently, "Hefei's got all the attributes investors need: land, energy and labor resources, rich education, ports nearby, talented workers, and a huge consumer market on its doorstep."[8] Unilever's migration reportedly slashed manufacturing costs by 25 percent.

With improving infrastructure in the form of the expressway system, high-speed trains, and airports, very little is lost in terms of transit time to major ports in the case of export. For domestic distribution points, more than 40 percent of China's consumer market is within 300 miles of Hefei, according to a study by the accounting and advisory firm KPMG. Recognizing these trends, Unilever is planning on doubling its production capacity in the next seven years.

In addition to Unilever, Hitachi, ABB, and Coca-Cola are just a few of the companies with factories in Hefei. The Continental Corporation opened its first manufacturing facility in Hefei in May 2011—its first in China. Built to supply the consumer auto market with an initial planned output of 4 million tires, the company has designed its manufacturing facility with expansion in mind, building facilities with a total planned output of 16 million tires.[9]

Most of these multinationals are located in a sprawling industrial park on the southwest side of the city. Known as the Hefei Economic and Technology Development Area (HETDA), the park covers 30 square miles and sits adjacent to the newly established international airport. In addition to the notable consumer powerhouses that are manufacturing in HETDA, automotive, heavy machinery, and other key industries are building up a productive base there.[10]

HETDA is not the only industrial park. The Hefei metropolitan area is dotted with the results of billions in government investment to produce a new economic, commercial center. Government representatives in Hefei have been very successful in attracting foreign investment and trumpeting the region as a center for business, even going so far as to say that it will represent a new Silicon Valley of China.[11]

As city siblings, Hefei and Columbus have their differences. Hefei is the younger, more muscular upstart in the family. The biggest difference is in population: Hefei's core city population is 3 million, compared to Columbus's population of less than 1 million. More than 59 million people reside in Anhui province. Growing infrastructure, a burgeoning multinational economic presence, and a steady supply of highly skilled and unskilled labor is raising Hefei's profile.

The *Economist*'s Intelligence Unit profiled five cities in China that represent the next wave of growth in China's economy.[12] Hefei is leading the pack. The province of Anhui includes five (including Hefei) of the country's fastest growing cities. Hefei was cited by a recent study as rising the fastest of any Chinese city in the area of business competitiveness.[13] Hefei's economy is surpassing economic growth in the coastal regions by around 70 percent. Data recently compiled by the Brookings Institution show Hefei to be among the top 10 fastest growing cities in the world.[14] The world's fastest growing cities are in central China and, like Hefei, away from the country's coastal regions.

All of these factors make up a formula for a fast-growing consumer market. As we saw in the regional segmentation analysis presented in Chapter 4, Anhui demonstrates the following:

- One of the fastest growth rates in urban disposable incomes.
- One of the largest populations of any provincial region.
- Dense, urban populations, with the city of Hefei at the forefront.

Within the class of the up-and-coming, fastest growing inland cities, Hefei is uniquely positioned in proximity to the already thriving consumer markets to the east. That influence helps it attract foreign investment and the growing manufacturing presence described earlier. Beginning in 2007, foreign direct investment exploded and more than doubled in the province, led by Hefei. With it came a commensurate growth in freight traffic. Before 2007, freight traffic growth in Anhui province was slow and steady. It more than doubled in 2007, from just over 500 million tons to more than 2,000 million tons through 2010.[15] Economic growth, foreign investment, and the growing presence of multinationals are just a few of the indicators that Hefei's economic growth is being turbocharged.

The city's unique position—and its turbocharged growth—is also driving a growing consumer culture, helping Hefei to establish itself as one of the next consumer gateway markets in China.

Big Retail Moves In

Consumerism and modern retail are on the rise in Hefei. As in other areas of the country, outdoor food stalls are being rapidly replaced as hypermarkets enter the local market and establish a foothold. Walmart has established up to five supercenters in the city. Carrefour has established a presence in the city as well. Starbucks opened its first store there in 2011; Hefei now has five Starbucks locations. The Chinese are acquiring the bitter taste of coffee, and more locations are bound to come (see sidebar, "Cups, Coffee, and Controversy"). Not that a cup of Starbucks is cheap—drinking one is Hefei is actually more expensive than in Columbus. A cup of Starbucks coffee can cost around $4.75.[16]

Cups, Coffee, and Controversy

Go local. That's what Starbucks Coffee has done as it seeks to expand and establish itself in China as its "second home" market. In the last few years, after anchoring itself in the mature economies of Beijing and Shanghai, the company decided to pioneer new store openings in the middle- and bottom-tier cities of inland markets. Pioneering inland, the consumer gateway cities of Yunnan and Hefei were one of the company's primary targets for store expansion (see the market analysis in Chapter 4 for why these cities are important). In August 2011, Starbucks opened its first store in Hefei and, in the brief span of little more than a year, grew to five stores in the city.

On opening day, the company unveiled locally branded Starbucks merchandise in the forms of cups and bottles. In addition to the iconic Starbucks logo, the company chose a drawing of Bao Zhen, a local historical figure from 1,000 years ago, and the words STARBUCKS HEFEI to announce its newly localized presence. Bao Zhen is somewhat of an ancient local celebrity; his temple is a leading tourist attraction in a city lacking big tourist sites. The items proved popular and sold quickly, contributing to a successful market launch that has grown in popularity.

Continued

But not everyone was pleased. To the probable surprise of Western executives, Bao Zhen still has some relatives in the area. His thirty-sixth-generation descendants raised objections in the media to the appropriation of the likeness of their distant relative, asserted copyright infringement, and threatened to sue. The subsequent national media coverage undoubtedly helped to stir the popularity pot for the store opening. Sometimes a little unanticipated controversy can help.

In cities like Shanghai, the company counted on foreign business travelers and clientele who have traveled abroad and are familiar with the brand to boost traffic and build awareness. That initial strategy proved successful and created a laboratory in which to experiment with product and service localization. Market-specific offerings, like a line of originally formulated green teas, followed. So did larger stores, when the company figured out that a larger percentage of its customers preferred to dine in relative to other markets.

Like every other successful venture in China, localization has been a central part of the strategy to reach consumers. The company also raised its level of customer service by fighting high employee turnover rates that are a regular part of doing business in China. Chinese employees are notoriously fickle. The company has invested heavily in employee training and inclusiveness.

All of these efforts are paying dividends for the company. From the starting point of opening its first store in 1999 to the company's ambitious expansion strategy in the last few years, the result is more than 500 stores in 42 cities across China. The goal is 1,500 stores by the year 2015.

That brings us back to the cups made specifically for Hefei's consumers and the controversy that came with them. Localization truly made its mark.

Sources: Compiled from *People's Daily*, a Starbucks press release, *China Daily USA*, and the *Wall Street Journal* [17]

The hypermarkets in Hefei are packed. These stores represent only the tip of the iceberg in consumer demand. In comparison, there are at least 11 Walmart supercenters in Columbus, Ohio, which has less than 20 percent of Hefei's metropolitan population. There are only 5 Walmarts in Hefei.

The market coverage gap widens considerably when we use Starbucks as the example. Dozens of purchase points for Starbucks are available to the 1 million Columbus area residents, but only five Starbucks stores serve Hefei's 5 million residents. This is a simple illustration of the tremendous upside consumer demand emerging in cities like Hefei. As the consumer class grows in numbers and spending power, the market coverage is extremely low.

Most of the hypermarkets and other examples of modern retail are located close to the inner ring of the city. The stores are clustered near heavily trafficked retail centers near the city center. None of the stores are farther than 6 miles from one another in a metro area that spans less than 3,000 square miles. The city's continued expansion creates untapped sources for additional consumers.

Domestic supermarkets and established ecommerce delivery networks step in to fill this void. There are thousands of small supermarkets across the city. Look at a map of Hefei and at the location of Walmart super-centers to understand the company's recent investment in Yihaodian, one of China's leading ecommerce players. Big hypermarket operators simply cannot execute a building strategy fast enough to meet the existing demand. Unless these companies develop new channels to fill in these underserved markets, the demand will be captured by the online competition. Hence the linking of Walmart and Yihaodian, which provides an avenue through an additional market channel to gain access to Hefei's expanding urban areas.

Big retail has no doubt arrived in Hefei, with growth continuing at a much faster pace in the more mature eastern markets. Now that modern retail has landed, the challenge will be to keep up with the demand and with rapid urbanization. To go deep into each of the next-generation markets like Hefei, retailers and manufacturers will win if they are able to use a combination of channels to maximize their reach.

Hefei is one of the gateway markets to the next generation of a growing consumer market. Chapter 4 outlined the analysis and segmentation of the locations that make up those gateways. They consist of four demand clusters and a framework for viewing the geographical hot spots of the emerging consumer demand. Chapter 5 described the channels to market being formed that act as entry points to these markets. Modern retail is rapidly moving in and establishing itself.

As the focus changes from entry to penetration, social media and the unique digital culture of the country are being embraced by companies that seek success. Establishing a direct relationship with consumers, influencing brand perception before consumers have made their purchasing decisions, and providing access through e-commerce will be critical. The distribution trends highlighted in Chapter 7 will complement these strategies. Companies are building up their own distribution infrastructures to address consumer anxiety about product safety and integrity.

No longer relegated to the few established markets on the coast, the market has broadened. All of these capabilities are coming together in a new go-to-market model to maximize consumer reach across the entire market.

Notes

1. "Statistical Summary," Ohio State University, August 23, 2012, www.osu.edu/osutoday/stuinfo.php.

2. Ohio State High Points, Ohio State University, August 6, 2012, www.osu.edu/highpoints/economicimpact.

3. Mark Brandau, "Why Chains Pick Columbus, Ohio, as Testmarket Target," *Nation's Restaurant News*, August 26, 2011.

4. Joseph Chen, Opening keynote address, China 2.0: Transforming Media and Commerce, Stanford Program on Regions of Innovation and Entrepreneurship conference, Stanford University, September 30, 2011, http://sprie.gsb.stanford.edu/events/china_20_transforming_media_and_commerce.

5. Geoff Dyer, "China: A New Core Rises," *Financial Times*, August 3, 2010; Jason Burke, "Welcome to China's Backwater—Population Five Million," *Guardian*, July 15, 2008.

6. Rob Gifford, *China Road: A Journey into the Future of a Rising Power* (New York: Random House, 2007).

7. "Hefei Overview," School of Information Science and Technology, August 23, 2012, http://en.sist.ustc.edu.cn/vistorinfo/201009/t20100906_34374.html.

8. Kevin Hamlin, "China's Inland Cities Power New Growth, Offsetting Slowing on Coast," *Bloomberg News*, April 10, 2012.

9. "Continental Officially Opens Its First Tire Plant in China," Continental Tire Company, press release, May 18, 2011, www.conti-online.com.

10. Hefei Economic and Technological Development Zone, National Economic and Technological Development Zones, www.china.org.cn/english/SPORT-c/75842.htm.

11. Gifford, *China Road*.

12. "Champs: China's Fastest-Growing Cities," *Economist*'s Intelligence Unit, 2010.

13. Zheng Weiling, "Hefei Tops Ranking of Central Chinese Cities' Competitiveness Rise," *Anhui News*, May 22, 2012, http://english.anhuinews.com/system/2012/05/22/004971566.shtml

14. Emilia Istrate and Carey Anne Nadeau, "Global Metro Monitor," Brookings Institution, November 30, 2012, www.brookings.edu/research/interactives/global-metro-monitor-3. This fascinating analysis shows that the fastest-growing cities in the world are located almost exclusively in China, whereas the slowest-growing cities in the world between 2011 and 2012 were in Europe. The corresponding map highlights the growth shift between the developed and emerging economies accelerated by the 2007 global downturn.

15. Deutche Bank Research, www.dbresearch.com.

16. Gao Changxin and Wang Jingshu, "No Coffee Mourning over Expensive Drinks in Starbucks," *China Daily*, February 9, 2012, http://usa.chinadaily.com.cn/business/2012-02/09/content_14565630.htm.

17. Huang Ying, "Starbucks China: Brewing Up a Success Coffee Story," *People's Daily*, March 1, 2012, http://english.peopledaily.com.cn/90778/7745001.html; "Starbucks Celebrates Its 500th Store Opening in Mainland China," Starbucks, press release, October 25, 2011, http://news.starbucks.com/article_display .cfm?article_id=580; "Baogong Has a Case against Popular Starbucks Coffee Mugs," *China Daily USA*, August 11, 2011, http://usa.chinadaily.com.cn/business/2011-08/11/content_13095568.htm; "Localization Fuels Starbucks' Success in China," *China Daily USA*, February 13, 2012, http://usa.chinadaily.com.cn/business/2012-02/13/content_14596142.htm; and "Starbucks to Brew a Bigger China Pot," *Wall Street Journal*, April 1, 2012, http://online.wsj.com/article/SB1 0001424052702303816504577317451106819664.html.

PART III

Forging Ahead

CHAPTER 9

Go Deep: The Emerging Go-to-Market Retail Model

The once geographically narrow, export-driven economic machine that launched China onto the world stage has given way. That era was born out of a wave of political campaigns that led to chaos and upended much of society. People starved in untold numbers. For those who survived the Great Leap Forward and the Cultural Revolution, there were repeated hardships, and education came to a halt. People went into hiding to escape persecution. Others were sent to rural camps where they were sentenced by the government to forced labor.

Throughout the 1980s, China rebuilt itself in the wake of these campaigns and launched one of the greatest economic revitalizations in history. Through the government-established Special Economic Zones, foreign investment flowed into the country in record numbers, primarily to the southern coastal regions, and China became the factory of the world.

This era was not without its costs. It spawned the largest human migration in history as poor, mostly agricultural, workers moved inland to work in the factories of the east. Families that were separated in previous generations because of politics were separated again because of economics. The factories driving the export model generated an environmental cost as well. Fueled by an insatiable demand for coal, China's industrial cities are covered in smog. The absence of regulation led to significant pollution. Countless lakes are polluted beyond the threshold of safe usage.

China is now turning away from that era to a broad-based consumer-driven economy. A new generation, unburdened by the past and more educated than their parents, is creating a new world. China's consumer economy is prefaced by an unprecedented infrastructure buildup, including a national expressway system and high-speed rail. What took the mature economies of Western Europe and the United States decades to do has been built in China within the span of a few years. New roads and infrastructure have made once faraway places closer and have created inland access to foreign investment and capital. Migration patterns to the coastal regions have decelerated. Urbanization within the country is increasing. Incomes are rising.

This new era, dominated by the Chinese consumer, will help to drive the next wave of global growth. It is both fast-moving and hard to predict. Lack of transparency relative to other markets means that response time is more limited. Trends appear to emerge faster in this market. In reality, a lack of information clouds the emerging trends, limiting clarity and market foresight, which subsequently decreases response time. Competitive actions are murky until after they have been executed.

The new consumer economy of China is composed of many individual markets. The export boom was largely homogeneous and isolated in the coastal east, whereas the broad-based consumer economy spans the country but differs in terms of how each region is poised to rise and fully participate. As detailed in Chapter 4, the many markets can be segmented into three large categories:

1. The coastal east is focused on the commercial centers of Shanghai and Guangdong to the south and the government capital of Beijing to the north. These areas are where the most competitive, mature markets are found. In the large centers, many markets are saturated, and consumers in the adjacent areas are coming into the fold.
2. Just to the west are regions that make up the emerging center. These areas, centered on emerging cities like Chongqing, Kunming, Hefei, and Chengdu, show the highest levels of urbanization and income growth in the country. If these names are not already familiar, they will become so in planning the next wave of global growth. They are where the growth of the consumer economy is the fastest and the new battles for market dominance are being fought.
3. The far western regions of the country are more isolated and have yet to show signs of full participation. Areas such as Tibet, Xinjiang, and Qinghai are characterized by disproportionate government investment, ethnic tension, dispersed populations, and stagnating income growth relative to other parts of the country.

The second area, the emerging center, has increasingly become the growth expansion target of modern retail. Having established themselves in the eastern capitals in the last decade, companies have recently turned their attention west to meet the ongoing demands for growth. Foreign hypermarkets like Walmart, Carrefour, and Tesco have expanded into cities in the emerging center to drive growth.

Consumers have been waiting. For them, modern retail is a new alternative that promises a safer, higher standard of living than the mom-and-pop stores and outdoor markets that dominated in the past. Emerging in the expansion parade are the luxury-brand manufacturers, selling consumers the aspiration for a better life through their own stores carefully chosen and established in inland capitals and regions of new consumer wealth. The domestic companies Suning and Gome have built a national network of stores focused on electronics and white goods. The ecommerce giants are there, too. Alibaba, and its Taobao mall, has leveraged the low-cost, government-subsidized postal service to reach broad swaths of the country.

The expansion of modern retail has been met with a simultaneous explosion in mobile device and Internet usage. A billion cell phone users and cheap, subsidized broadband access means that the most populous nation on earth is now one of the most literate online. This population is the most engaged, unique, and interactive user of the Internet, using social media at a higher level than any other market. Chinese users actively use the Internet as a medium of expression and opinion at unprecedented levels. The Internet's influence on purchasing and brand influence begins sooner and goes deeper than anywhere else. Companies seeking broader consumer reach start with engaging consumers in China's unique, digital world.

As modern retail expands into the western inland provinces, new demands to advance the distribution infrastructure have emerged. These infrastructure advances were pioneered in an experimental, do-it-yourself fashion. As a result, different distribution models exist. Retailers are moving toward centralized direct buying with larger suppliers. The legacy system of multiple intermediaries is being replaced by a more streamlined system. The recent emergence of an outsourced, third-party distribution industry is providing more scale economies and reach, but gaps remain. The stark realities of China's food safety crisis are, more than ever before, driving new solutions to big issues like the absence of refrigerated trucking at an industry level.

All of these trends, happening simultaneously and interacting with one another, are creating a new go-to-market model for the retail and consumer goods market. Understanding this emerging model can lead to insights on how consumers will purchase goods in the future and how the goods will reach the consumers. For retailers and manufacturers alike, this understanding will provide a template for the emerging landscape and indicate how to compete within the time horizon of the next five years.

The Emerging Go-to-Market Model

The go-to-market model emerging in China, highlighted in Figure 9.1, is based on both current market realities and the urgent, competitive drive to maximize consumer reach. It is based on the following three layers, which can be viewed as a sequential approach:

1. Organizing and monitoring market success at a provincial level.
2. Using a provincial model in an expanding-out approach that targets the highest areas of growth.
3. Using an expanding-in strategy based on a multichannel approach that will be the standard as companies pursue all avenues to reach consumers and blunt their competitors.

Targeting Demand Clusters and Expanding Out

The emerging go-to-market model starts with a realization that it will be organized around province-specific strategies. To some, this may appear counterintuitive. Many will point to clear trends toward a more centralized distribution and marketing model. Clearly, more sophisticated retailers are indeed moving away from store-specific buying. The transition from a growth-at-all-costs focus to one of increasing operational scale will lead to more efficiency and, yes, greater centralization. However, efforts in the past few years toward centralization appear to have been a bit too ambitious and have therefore been scaled back. Operational efficiencies and the implementation of capabilities leading to a greater operational scale will take time. Meanwhile, other trends in the market

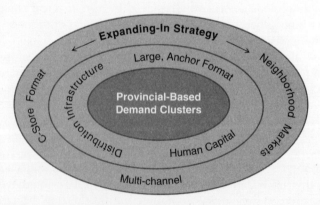

FIGURE 9.1 China's Emerging Go-to-Market Model

will promote a province-based go-to-market model. These trends include the following:

- Ongoing regulation and government policy will be administered at the provincial level. Not all retail and trade legislation is executed at the provincial level. E-commerce is a notable exception in which policy is dictated nationally. Yet a vast number of regulations, such as site licenses, will most likely remain at the provincial level. A company's efforts to build relationships and influence government policy will have to be heavily emphasized at this level.
- Competition is likely to remain specific to provincial regions. The legacy department store channels remain a vital force in the market and are largely centered in their home regions. These companies will strongly defend their home turf and create different competitive dynamics in their respective provincial regions.
- The continued focus on product safety translates into a greater emphasis on local execution. Many direct sourcing programs have a local orientation. In the meantime, locally based sourcing will facilitate closing the gaps in refrigerated trucking, which will take time.
- Road congestion prevents reliable replenishment times across long distances. Until the high-speed rail infrastructure transfers human traffic from the roads and the country's reliance on coal as the primary energy source ebbs, the country's current rail network will operate at full capacity and will not provide a more cost-effective alternative to roads. This will mean increased traffic congestion. With car ownership becoming more common, transit times in urban centers will remain uncertain. The country's toll system on expressways and the provinces' specific regulations will make interprovincial shipping a continued challenge.

Last, and perhaps most important, consumer tastes vary significantly among the provincial markets of the country. Different climates, microcultures, and historical isolation create a much broader spectrum of consumer preferences in China than in other markets. Certainly centralization will increase in the operations of retailers and manufacturers. It's almost impossible for it not to do so, given the extreme levels of decentralization operating in the market today. For the foreseeable future, balance will be required, and that balance will be made by organizing around provinces and provincial clusters.

Chapter 4 introduced a supporting fact base and a framework for how companies can start thinking about competition and market access at a provincial level. For companies that have yet to move west into broader inland markets, this analysis presents an approach for selecting the provinces that align with the highest value-creating potential. For those companies that have begun the process of penetrating inland markets, the analysis also presents a framework for how to monitor market conditions and supply market demand by segmenting the market into the following four demand clusters:

1. **The Guangdong cluster.** This group of provinces is the heart of the export centers of the southeast. These are dense, mature, thriving consumer markets with relatively robust infrastructure.
2. **The Beijing cluster.** This group of provinces includes the government capital, Beijing, and the nearby industrial center of Tianjin. These strong markets are joined by neighboring provinces that will become part of the consumer economy as income levels increase.
3. **The Chengdu cluster.** Centered in the breakout metropolitan cities of Chengdu and Chongqing, this group of provinces will lead consumer growth in the market.
4. **The Anhui cluster.** Located in the Pearl River Delta, this group of provinces lies just inland, up the Yangtze River beyond Shanghai. This group of provinces is centered in Anhui, a province with many of the country's fastest growing cities. Anhui has a dense population, a rising consumer class, and an established infrastructure that enables more efficient distribution.

Using this framework and its macroeconomic consumer trends as a base, companies can establish and monitor an anchor strategy to establish a presence in target areas. As modern retail has begun sweeping across the inland regions, many retailers have established an effective anchor presence in the high-target cities within each of these demand clusters. International hypermarkets and luxury-branded manufacturers have established a store base in the middle tier, mainly provincial capitals, and the bottom tier, other large cities, in these areas. The implementation of this step brings distribution capability and human capital into these targeted demand clusters.

Expanding In

As modern retail continues to establish itself in high-target inland areas by targeting the right provinces, opportunity creates further challenge. For retailers of fast-moving consumer goods, a few anchor stores in a large provincial capital create an initial huge spike in demand. Given the huge scale of these cities, an anchor strategy of a few stores covers only a sliver of the entire addressable market. Competitors immediately emerge in other areas of these large metropolitan cities to take market share. E-commerce companies establish delivery networks to do the same.

To combat this, multichannel retailing will become an essential component of the go-to-market model to maximize growth potential for retailers.
Virtually every major retailer and many branded manufacturers will engage
in multichannel delivery systems. For hypermarkets, an initial presence
that includes large-format stores will be followed by smaller formats like
convenience stores, which will be established closer to residential communities. The integration of brick-and-mortar stores and online consumer
activity will accelerate.

With market coverage and retail concentration low, driving growth to
increase market reach will remain the primary objective. A coordinated
multichannel approach to reaching consumers will be an integral part of
reaching that objective. As an extension, retailers and manufacturers will
use a social media strategy that is locally based. Localized promotion strategies will build demand, and locally based participatory communities will
be formed to increase brand loyalty and influence brand perception. All
retailers will use e-commerce and the promise of local delivery to fight
for more market coverage. In the next few years, this emerging model will
result in very dense distribution networks across the country and escalating
competition.

One way to view the emerging go-to-market trends is to view them as
a set of sequentially developed capabilities. These capabilities will probably
be developed by region as retailers and manufacturers continue to target
new demand clusters and expand inland. Figure 9.2 is a representation of
how these capabilities might develop for brick-and-mortar retailers. This
view can be used as an overlay on each of the demand clusters to chart
consumer and market progress in each targeted area in the broader market.

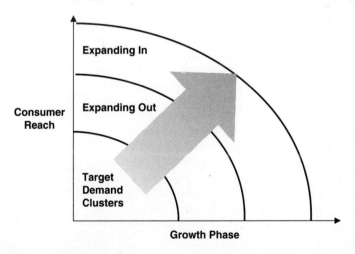

FIGURE 9.2 Go-to-Market Road Map

The Implications for Retailers and Manufacturers

The go-to-market road map is a high-level picture of the evolving market. It encapsulates the current and emerging trends across the market and shows how they can begin to be interpreted and prioritized into a go-to-market plan.

Table 9.1 lists some of the key capabilities required in each phase of the emerging model. The first phase, target demand clusters, encompasses rigorous analytical planning capabilities. These are then institutionalized to monitor ongoing developments in areas like consumer spending and income growth, specific to each demand cluster. The expanding-out phase involves the front market and consumer-facing capabilities involved in establishing a market presence. They include capabilities in product selection and planning, consumer research and segmentation, store layout, and pricing. The expanding-in phase includes the capabilities for expansion within demand clusters once a market presence has been established, including format expansion, the utilization of localized social media, and the establishment of delivery networks as the vital complement to e-commerce.

TABLE 9.1 Organizational Capabilities

Growth Phase	Illustrative Capabilities
Target demand clusters	▪ Economic analysis ▪ Consumer segmentation ▪ Product mapping
Expanding out	▪ Site selection and building ▪ Merchandising and assortment ▪ Planogramming and space planning ▪ Product planning ▪ Pricing ▪ Distribution planning ▪ Labor management ▪ Vendor management ▪ Replenishment ▪ Store operations ▪ Customer service ▪ Marketing and advertising
Expanding in	▪ E-commerce strategy and execution ▪ Social media strategy and execution ▪ Format expansion ▪ Multichannel integration ▪ Local last-mile distribution ▪ Local competitive and market intelligence

The larger question about these capabilities is where they might reside in the organization. Much has been written about the evolution toward centralization in China's consumer goods market. Indeed, many companies are finding continued, sustained profitability to be a challenge. Given the economic headwinds elsewhere, the approach of seeking growth at the expense of profitability is increasingly seen as a luxury rather than a sound, sustainable strategy.

That emerging consensus is adding impetus to greater efficiencies that come from more centralized operations. Yet plans in the past five years to centralize operations have been moderated. Any discussion of greater centralization should start with the realization that operations are much more decentralized relative to other markets. For the majority of the industry, the pendulum is squarely at the decentralization end, and there is certainly room for improvement.

Like anything else, the correct answer lies in striking a balance between market need and the cost imperative. The level of each demand cluster provides a threshold between the front-market, consumer-facing capability and other business operational processes. For reasons such as different consumer tastes, key activities affecting consumer satisfaction, and market trends, these activities will most likely gravitate more toward a local and demand cluster level. Merchandising, store presentation, pricing, and localized promotions are all examples of business operations that can benefit from being closer to end markets at the provincial level.

Another reason for this likely direction is the lack of market data available in China. Being closer to end markets provides more timely feedback. As noted earlier, Walmart frequently sends its store managers out to local outdoor "wet" markets to investigate prices and assess whether any changes should be made in their stores. This is just one example of the type of local knowledge and decision making that will be required in the foreseeable future.

While customer-facing processes will emphasize local decision making and coordination, other business capabilities requiring a specialized scale will benefit from a more centralized approach. Retailers' and manufacturers' approach to e-commerce and social media is a great example of a capability in this category. Providing a common strategy with centrally developed tools, platforms, and guidelines will benefit the customer-facing parts of the organization at the demand cluster level.

In many instances, and Internet strategy is one of them, companies will be forging totally new capabilities, not ones that can be referenced and then imported from other markets. This kind of innovation is likely to move toward centralization because of its highly specialized nature.

Another example is distribution. Setting up distribution networks that can be responsive within each demand cluster will require deep expertise, but they will provide a strategy and an implementation approach across the market as the presence in new geographical areas (e.g., demand clusters) is established. Figure 9.3 illustrates the capabilities that will tend toward either regional execution or greater centralization.

For manufacturers, the emerging go-to-market model implies different ways to serve their retailer customers than the current model in more developed markets does. In the more developed markets of the United States and Western Europe, retailer consolidation has led to the concentration of resources and an increased investment in a smaller number of key accounts. It has also meant a greater depth of specialization and more corporate focus as the centralization of business operations within retailers has taken hold. Increased IT capability, the implementation of shared service models, and a desire for greater management control has resulted in business operations like pricing, promotion, and merchandising, moving out of individual markets into the corporate realm.

Syndicated data providers such as IRI and Nielsen provide timely, accurate data that are aggregated at the full market level. This provides a window into the pulse of the market to enable a rapid sensing of market changes in demand and consumer preference. It also facilitates specialization at the corporate center. As manufacturers evolve in this direction, the gap between current capability and capability in these developed markets will require a more decentralized approach. Manufacturers will need resources in each of the demand clusters.

Manufacturers can use this go-to-market framework to discern the stages of market penetration by demand cluster for their downstream retailer

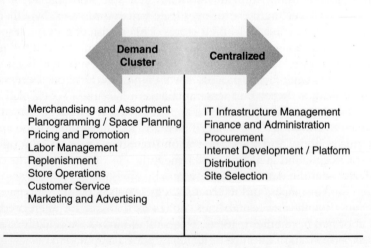

FIGURE 9.3 Striking the Right Balance between Centralization and Local Demand Cluster Markets

customers. They can assess the degree of market coverage for each retail partner, the best way to assist the retailer in ways that improve their own competitive position, and the best resource profile among individual account teams.

IT as an Enabler

In Boulder, Colorado, a small start-up company holds the keys to understanding the pulse of the Chinese consumer. Gnip is a small company formed to collect, consolidate, and distribute social media data. The company's flagship offering is its agreement with Twitter to resell aggregated Twitter postings to companies. The service has generated strong interest. "Our biggest use case is brands wanting to know everything that's said about them in social," said the company's president and chief operating office.[1]

The promise is certainly inspiring. Access to social media data portends the capability to obtain instant feedback on consumer responses to products and fast-changing preferences. The *Wall Street Journal* recently offered an illustration of the inherent potential of aggregating social media data. In August 2011, an earthquake occurred in Virginia that was felt throughout the Northeast. Knowledge of the earthquake was transmitted through Twitter almost instantly, with thousands of messages generated by people as they experienced the earthquake's tremors. The timeliness of this feedback outpaced the seismometers of the U.S. Geological Survey by a full 20 minutes.[2]

That example, translated into the language of consumer behavior, illustrates the potential of aggregating and analyzing social media data. Direct consumer data trump government data every time; they are more timely and come direct from the source. In China, government-released data are sparse and received with a high degree of skepticism by many. The habit in the old days of inflating report numbers at the provincial level to please the bureaucrats in the central government has not completely been extinguished. To understand China's macroeconomic direction, economists often look to electrical output as a leading indicator. If manufacturing plants and distribution centers aren't running, the theory goes, similar trends in economic output will follow. It makes sense, and it's an example of the creativity involved in figuring out economic and consumer trends in the midst of data sources that are few and far between.

Enter Gnip. In April 2012, the company announced a partnership with Sina Weibo to collect, consolidate, and resell Weibo's data. Suddenly, brand manufacturers and retail companies could gain access to the aggregated data posted by Sina's 300 million users. Access to Sina's data was the number one request from Gnip's customers, according to the company's president.[3]

That certainly seems to be an understatement. Chapter 6 outlined how critical and unique China's digital world is in understanding and reaching

Chinese consumers. Add to that the multichannel evolution that is occurring in the market today. Choice for consumers in densely populated urban centers is increasing rapidly. Yet the ability for retailers and brand manufacturers to differentiate is challenging, primarily because timely and accurate consumer data are often hard to come by.

That is beginning to change with offerings by companies like Gnip. New, rapidly developed insights into consumers, combined with consumer and market functions organized close to distinct demand cluster markets, offer companies high potential to customize their products and tailor their offerings in an appropriately differentiated way.

Let's say that I am a luxury-brand manufacturer and I want to get access to all of the message postings on Sina Weibo. I can now do that through Gnip's partnership. But here is the problem: Companies like Gnip only offer companies *access* to the data. Doing the analysis that generates the consumer insights is up to you. Your company will need a separate set of software tools, a lot more servers to store all that data, and skilled workers to perform the analysis. Thus, the promise of gaining access to social media data only leads to further challenges.

A more established data company that provides access to direct consumer data is the Nielsen Company. Anyone who operates in the consumer industry is probably familiar with Nielsen, a pioneer of the syndicated data industry. This industry follows the business model in which retail data are collected, consolidated, aggregated, and then sold to companies seeking consumer insight—mostly the consumer packaged goods manufacturers.

Any sales and marketing executive of consumer packaged goods knows Nielsen data well. Its solutions are staples in developed consumer markets today and a central part of any sales and marketing decision making. Tracking sales of new products, changes to market share, and promotional performance are just a few of the activities on which manufacturers rely and for which they use syndicated data. Nielsen has invested heavily in China in the last five years, seeking to provide a much-needed data visibility into consumer preference and product sales.

In 2007, Nielsen was able to provide its customers product sales data at an aggregated, geographical level for four defined regions, reportedly covering 45 percent of consumer sales. These regions were in the eastern and central parts of the country, excluding the poorer provinces in the far west.

In 2011, Nielsen reached a coverage of approximately 60 percent of consumer sales reported at the provincial level.[4] These are, of course, great strides, providing a visibility that most manufacturers need and do not have. (Luxury-brand companies usually have much of their own sales data because of vertical integration and ownership of stores, but they lack a total market picture.) Data can be accessed and mapped by product at the provincial level, the demand cluster level, and the country level. It's important to realize, however, that the accuracy of this data has a much higher variability than in more mature markets.

Nielsen cannot establish data-sharing partnerships with every retailer, and such arrangements are new for the larger, domestically owned chains. In these cases, Nielsen most likely relies more on data extrapolation and human labor collection systems than it does in the developed markets with more consolidated retail and pervasive point-of-sale systems. Nonetheless, both Nielsen and companies like Gnip enable brand manufacturers and retailers to obtain a timelier and much closer view of consumer demand and behavior than ever before.

As China's go-to-market consumer base evolves, companies are seeking new capabilities like these in order to gain an edge. Four enterprise software segments are showing the highest growth rates and largest revenue in the market: enterprise resource planning, customer relationship management, supply chain management, and business intelligence. Each is forecast to grow more than 18 percent annually and to double in market size in the next few years.[5] Gartner, a technology market research firm, reports that the highest priorities in consumer industries for IT support are in the areas of supply chain, data analytics, and customer relationship management.[6]

Just like other industries, the IT industry is composed of domestic companies that do well in the middle and bottom tiers of the market as well as that of bigger, foreign-run companies that serve multinationals. Companies like IBM, Oracle, and SAP are making large investments in the market, hoping to succeed by supporting companies in creating the necessary capabilities for expansion.

The picture painted by the market is of an evolving consumer go-to-market model that extends broadly across channels and deep through distribution. In chosen markets, companies will use their strengths in their core formats to enter and then expand. Brick-and-mortar retailers will use this format as entry vehicles but then leverage partnerships or buyouts to expand into other formats and use e-commerce to close market gaps and beat their competitors. E-commerce companies like Alibaba will establish residential distribution networks to seek market dominance before their brick-and-mortar competitors are able to attain total coverage.

The race is actively underway. Its pace will be determined by larger, short-term economic growth rates. Slower economic growth rates may translate into a higher importance being placed on profitability and the luxury to move more deliberately. Faster economic growth may translate into what we have seen in the last few years, which is expansion driven by revenue and greater market reach at breakneck speeds.

The expansion and buildup of a modern consumer economy is only a matter of timing. The track has been laid.

Notes

1. David Carr, "Gnip Now Shares Social Sentiments from China," *Information Week*, April 10, 2012, www.informationweek.com/thebrainyard/news/social_ networking_consumer/232900045/gnip-now-shares-social-sentiments-from-china.

2. Robert Lee Holz, "Decoding Our Chatter," *Wall Street Journal*, October 1, 2011.

3. David F. Carr, "Gnip Now Shares Social Sentiments from China," *Information Week*, April 10, 2012.

4. "Nielsen Investor Deep Dive," Nielsen, September 13, 2011, www.nielsen.com.

5. Hai Hong Swinehart and Yanna Dharmasthira, "Competitive Landscape: Enterprise Application Software Market, China," *Gartner Research Service*, August 25, 2011.

6. Tina Tang, "Market Trends: IT Services, Asia/Pacific, 2011–2012," *Gartner Research Service*.

CHAPTER 10

The New Export Machine

For those in the mature, developed markets of the West, more innovation is coming your way. China's export machine used to involve just physical goods; that was the old world. The new world places intellectual capital and innovation into the export mix. New ideas, processes, and products invented to tap the growing consumer market in China are increasingly becoming global. Here is why:

- **A dense market.** China's consumer market, especially in the established coastal regions, is dense and competitive. This is driving new ways to reach consumers.
- **A growth in innovation.** China's innovation capacity is undergoing significant growth, led by a vast and educated labor force supported by the strength of government investment.
- **More constraints.** As the pressure for growth drives companies inland, market constraints spur further innovation. Although much progress in infrastructure has been made, distribution systems often don't work. Physical stores cannot be built fast enough to ensure market coverage. These constraints lead to innovations born out of necessity.
- **The market pace.** China is a more iterative market in terms of new product launches. The cycle time from ideation to market launch is faster, followed by rapid improvement cycles after the initial consumer response. The careful, deliberate, top-down approach used by multinationals in the past is rapidly being replaced in all markets by faster development cycles that force a quicker pace.
- **A broader price ladder.** As the search to reach more Chinese consumers continues, companies are increasing their commitment to tailor products to lower-income consumers. The "bottom of the pyramid" opportunity, articulated so well by the late author C. K. Prahalad, is now becoming a reality.[1]

Two Examples of China-Based Innovation: Kraft Foods and the Coca-Cola Company

One example in the increasing innovation coming from China lies in the iconic Oreo cookie, manufactured and marketed by Kraft Foods.[2] Anyone of a certain age whose youth was spent living in one of Kraft's established markets knows the Oreo well. For many, consuming the product is forever imprinted on the brain. Oreo is the product leader in the Kraft portfolio and extending its success into the Chinese market seemed a natural, almost intuitive, way to establish itself in China. The iconic product landed in new territory in 1996, when Kraft Foods entered the Chinese market. Up until the last few years, the Oreo cookie stacked on the shelves of Chinese stores was identical to the product sold in Kraft's home market of the United States. In fact, the products were the same in every way with the exception of Chinese packaging. Forever a staple of American culture, the Oreo did not catch on in the Chinese market. For as much admiration Chinese consumers devote to American brands, preference for American taste buds can be a different story. A few years ago in response, Kraft made the investment to study the Chinese consumer's reaction to the iconic product. They found a mixed reaction to the taste. Consumers apparently did not know what to make of the combination of the bitter cookie and the extra sweet creamy center. As a result of consumer insights obtained by the company, the product's formula and presentation were redesigned for the Chinese market. Out went the cookie design entirely, replaced by what can best be described as a cookie stick.

The product reformulation was combined with a focus on the consumer experience in an advertising campaign to encourage consumers to take another look at Kraft's flagship product. The targeted consumer experience in the advertising campaign was the dunk: the familiar practice of submerging the product in milk to produce a satisfying taste. Specifically, Kraft's advertising campaign used in conjunction with the relaunch showed young children teaching their parents and grandparents the virtues of the Oreo dunk. The results were magical, and sales of the product skyrocketed. Oreo is now the best-selling cookie in the market.[3]

Kraft Foods is now extending the same process to all of its products. It will take the same kind of concerted effort to radically localize the products in Kraft's China-based portfolio for the company's market success to continue. China's market, especially in snack foods, is crowded, fragmented, and full of domestic competition. The top 10 sellers of snack foods are dominated by domestic producers.

Kraft is now introducing a host of new flavors in its Ritz cracker line that would not be recognized in Kraft's home market, like Beef Stew and Spicy Chicken.[4] The company's new product push is being supported by a large research facility in China focused on new product formulations for the domestic market. As the company radically localizes, it is also expanding its distribution and marketing. Kraft is exporting the new Oreo to other markets, such as Canada and Australia.

Kraft's journey—from pushing unchanged products at entry to localizing and then extending—is a common one that many companies have used to take advantage of market lessons and increase their success. What is perhaps a surprise to these companies is that these new products, designed for the Chinese consumer, are increasingly being exported to other markets as part of each company's innovation path.

Mature markets have suffered from a scarcity of major innovations by many of the established leaders in the market. The new product formulation process in consumer packaged goods is usually ruled by the line extension, which emphasizes incremental changes in an established product. These "new products" are not really new, but instead contain small changes as a way of seeking new purchases on the margins of an established customer base. The formula works for small, incremental growth, but it siphons off resources and the capability to produce more radical redesigns, such as those now happening in these categories in China. Both refreshed products and entirely new products can be tested in China and exported to tap further growth opportunities (see Figure 10.1).

Another great example of China-based innovation is provided by the Coca-Cola Company. The company's top-selling fruit-based drink is Pulpy, which was developed and launched in China in 2005 and exported across Asia and Latin America. By 2012, the product had generated a billion dollars in annual revenue, joining only a dozen other Coke products in achieving that milestone.

Although Pulpy is now one of Coca-Cola's emerging flagship products, it is not yet available in the United States or Western Europe. It is the only product on this exclusive list of Coke's billion-dollar brands not available for

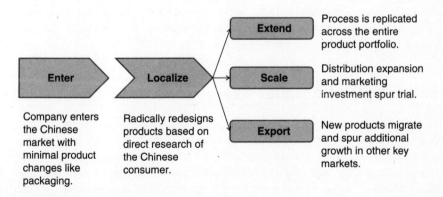

FIGURE 10.1 The Innovation Path

sale in these countries. The key to the success was to first tap the Chinese consumer opportunity, then follow with a rapid product rollout to other countries.

"China is going to be used as a test base for new food and beverage products because of its huge and diverse population," said Marie Jiang, a retail analyst with Pacific Epoch. "If it can succeed in China, chances are it will overseas."[5] Following the success of Pulpy, Coca-Cola is broadening the localized redesign of its products across its portfolio. It launched Sprint Tea in 2011, which is a combination of green tea and Coke.

If these products are successful in the Chinese market, we can expect them to be rapidly exported in what is becoming a new recipe in global innovation. This recipe includes a research and development (R&D) base in China, locally redesigned products across the portfolio, the use of the Chinese market as a test market, and rapid geographical expansion.

These examples of new products from Kraft and Coke illustrate the changing picture of innovation. Neither of these examples would have been likely to happen in the previous multinational approach of top-down, Western-located innovation. A more decentralized, globalized innovation capability is being created, and China's innovation capacity is catching up fast to that of the rest of the world.

Fortune 500 companies now have more than 98 R&D facilities in China.[6] The Organization for Economic Cooperation reported that R&D spending is falling among its member countries; it decreased 4.5 percent in 2009. China is upending the trend, with R&D spending increasing about 30 percent in 2010. China's global share of total R&D spending is on the rise, climbing from 7 percent in 2004 to 13 percent in 2009.[7] And more of this investment (60 percent) is being spent by private companies.[8]

To support the increased spending, China's higher education system is graduating more than 2 million engineers per year, more than five times the rate of the United States.[9] Kraft's and Coke's commercial successes show the early returns stemming from these investments. These two examples of China-based innovation showcase the rising trend of innovation moving from East to West.

Switching the Innovation Gear

This innovation trend is providing a new addition to the management lexicon: *reverse innovation*. General Electric's chief consultant on innovation, noted academic Vijay Govindarajan, started to see early signs of this trend along with its potential to impact GE's market share. His work with GE dug deep into the efforts of the company to develop products suitable for the "bottom of the pyramid." According to his research and experience, products targeting these markets must be radically simplified and redesigned, with the following characteristics:

- Highly portable, to encourage use in multiple settings by multiple people.
- Easy to use, given that hands-on training and white-glove service may not be available.
- Very affordable.

The author found that an innovation approach with these objectives is the inverse of the innovation practiced in the West in the past few generations. For Western markets, comparisons of marginal cost and marginal benefit have been the guide—in other words, adjustments to the margin of a solid product foundation. For instance, what is the cost of a small incremental feature, such as an additional button on a camcorder or an additional flavor in a cookie? How does this compare with the market advantage available with this change, perhaps through securing additional shelf space at a retailer or being able to charge a higher price? And so it has been in the laboratories of the developed markets.

Mr. Govindarajan found through his work that the underlying assumptions of current innovation were often ill-suited for emerging markets like China. Existing product platforms were too often built for different customers with different needs. It's impossible to have innovation success on the margins when you need to rethink the foundation. He needed a new model to drive more success at GE. In the book he recently coauthored, *Reverse Innovation: Create Far from Home, Win Everywhere*, he outlines examples of what that new model looks like and how it can be put in practice.

One of the best examples is a new product launched by GE that "fundamentally rethinks the price-performance curve."[10] The company developed an ultrasound product, Vscan, that is portable, can be used with little training, and is offered at a fraction of the cost of similar products in its portfolio. It's perhaps no surprise that the product has migrated into more mature markets and enjoyed success there as well.[11] And so the term *reverse innovation* is entering the mainstream of management vocabulary.

Frugal innovation is another term often used to describe the new nature of innovation that has taken root in China. The focal point here is the notion that all the features and functions added to a product have to be rethought and often rejected under new design objectives and new consumer value propositions.

The growing research on innovation in China is a source of validation that something new is happening. Yet the emphasis on these new schools of thought seem to be almost exclusively focused on product innovation. What is seen today in China is innovation across the spectrum of business operations that will dramatically affect how goods are developed, sold, delivered, and consumed by people everywhere.

In addition to product innovation, two additional areas of innovation stand out as having a great potential to expand beyond China's borders.

Distribution Innovation

One of the areas in which China acts as an innovation incubator is distribution. Distribution innovation is targeting greater market reach and changing the way consumers receive the goods they buy.

The virtual grocery store now present in the subways of Shanghai is a good example of distribution innovation. Highlighted in Chapter 7, this new concept was developed by Tesco, piloted in South Korea, and rapidly expanded into Shanghai, and it is now spreading around the globe. How and why has this happened? First, the virtual grocery store is a distribution innovation that captures incremental demand by placing more points of purchase in the market. Creating new paths to purchase will be critical in the austere economic conditions of the West. Second, it involves the use of a smartphone. A consumer needs a smartphone in order to download the application that enables order and delivery to his or her home. In the big cities of China, smartphone use is pervasive, and its adoption rate is ahead of that in Western markets. The lessons learned and the innovations sparked by smartphone usage can be transferred as consumers in developed markets approach higher rates of smartphone adoption.

It is starting to happen. Tesco launched a version of the virtual grocery store in London's Gatwick Airport in August 2012. The company, trying to rejuvenate success in its home market, imported the idea as a trial. Currently, about 50 percent of consumers use a smartphone in Britain. By 2016, close to all of them will use one. "There is a huge amount of money being spent by customers using smart phones on the go.... This is bringing in new incremental business," Tesco's director of Internet retailing commented regarding the launch of the store.[12]

This is likely to be just the start of the expansion of this new concept. The grocery business is one of the toughest, most competitive industries. Razor-thin margins mean a ruthless fight for market share. This distribution model now provides the opportunity to reach more consumers at the point of need without the large investment required to build a store. Much of the concept is software, so an initial investment motivates multiple rollouts to recoup investment. These trends, along with flat demand in other markets that add a sense of urgency for something new, will lead to the rapid deployment of this concept. So yes, expect to see smartphone-enabled virtual stores coming to a train station near you soon.

Residential Distribution

Another area of innovation is the establishment of pervasive dense networks of urban residential distribution. These are becoming a reality everywhere in China. As described in Chapter 7, the retail market cannot build stores fast enough to cover the inland markets where toeholds are being established. The same can be said for the growing sprawling metroplexes in the coastal regions. As urban centers in China grow to become the largest in the world, urban residential distribution networks are taking hold as a way to enable higher market coverage. And the concept is being exported.

Outside China, the best example of increased dense residential distribution as a tenet of corporate strategy is Amazon. Amazon is making this kind of distribution capability a reality in the United States. Located in Seattle, Washington, Amazon is, of course, the original online retailer. Its story is now the stuff of legend. Founder Jeff Bezos left a promising career in investment banking, exchanging relative stability for his dream of setting up a store on the Internet that, back in the mid-1990s, was a new and unproven technology. Over the years, after incredible success, Amazon expanded from its original product category of books to cover virtually every conceivable type of product that can be shipped parcel post.

Now Bezos is intending to shift the competitive ground yet again—this time through distribution capability. Perhaps as a result of seeing the developments by the leading e-commerce players in China, Bezos is building a large network of distribution centers across the United States. Once this buildup is complete, the largest metropolitan areas in the United States will be reachable within a day. If the company is successful in executing the strategy, Amazon "will be the dominant retailer in the decade to come," according to an analyst from the market research company Forrester.[13]

Because online retailers are often able to offer lower prices to consumers than those found in physical stores, the only disadvantage the online retailers have in relation to their store-based competitors is timeliness. Some consumers place a value on immediacy: being able to find the product and possess it at once. But what if they could order online in the morning and have the product delivered in the afternoon? The answer seems obvious. If consumers can tap the convenience of online shopping, benefit from its price advantages, *and* receive the purchased goods within a day, then more consumers will be likely to switch more of their purchasing to this channel. Amazon is counting on this to deliver significant share gains.

China's development of these networks was the preface to Amazon's strategy. With modern retail lacking a significant brick-and-mortar presence in many Chinese cities, online retailers have invested and created dense residential distribution capabilities to take market share before more competition arrives. Amazon, the original e-commerce store, probably learned this from its eastern counterpart, Alibaba.

If so, it certainly is a representative example of the larger story about the flow of innovation now spreading from East to West. Jack Ma, the founder of Alibaba, was a teacher in Seattle during the late 1990s, only to return to China and launch what became the dominant power in the fastest growing e-commerce market in the world. Now his company is the source of new innovation traveling back the other way.

China's fast market pace and its expansion constraints have created a hotbed of distribution innovation. That innovation is creating incremental demand and new ways to reach the country's consumer base. It's no longer a question of *when* those innovations will start to affect developed markets. They already have.

Digital Culture

Much of the innovation in China today stems from the country's digital culture. Examples of this can be found by looking at how the country's use of social media and the Internet has evolved. As noted in Chapter 6, China's consumers are much more interactive and networked through the Internet than users in other markets. This has made cyberspace an incubator of innovation. Desktop-to-mobile integration, the preponderance of games on social media sites (often coined with the term *gamification*), innovative ways to connect users within their network of friends, and products that promote shared experiences are all characteristics of China's Internet that will migrate to other markets. As they do, branded consumer companies and retailers should be prepared to respond, shifting the strategies used in the Chinese market to the rest of the world.

An example of this kind of exportable innovation is Renren's recently launched version of user-customized Internet radio. Similar to applications like Pandora, this product enables its users to establish a profile of the types of music and artists they prefer. Then, through the magic of the Internet, these preferences translate almost immediately into an individually customized radio station for the user. Renren's offering goes one step further than others by allowing that customized radio station to be shared with and listened to simultaneously by a group of users who befriend one another on the Renren platform. This difference highlights the higher level of interactivity and community of the Chinese Internet, which can be exploited for growth into other markets.

Applying lessons from China's mobile Internet users also holds potential. Between 2009 and 2012, mobile access to the Internet has increased from almost zero to 10 percent of the total global Internet traffic.[14] It's certainly much more in China. Many Western companies are getting caught a bit flat-footed as more and more traffic moves to mobile platforms, and they are pushing hard to increase their number of mobile users and the money they get from them. Facebook's mobile efforts in particular have been criticized as being merely an extension of its desktop application, with few customizations or bottom-up designs for the mobile experience.

The large China-based social networking companies like Renren and Tencent have made great strides in these areas. Tencent built its mobile product from scratch. The company launched Weixin, a mobile chat platform that seamlessly integrates photo and audio sharing. The service has garnered more than 100 million users since its launch in 2011.[15] The chat platform is already crossing borders as WeChat. Since Weixin's success in Tencent's home market, WeChat's target markets have included Indonesia, Singapore, Taiwan, Hong Kong, Thailand, Malaysia, and Vietnam. As of October 2012, the user base for WeChat outside China was on the verge of outpacing the user base in China. With open integration to Facebook, Twitter, and other social media applications, WeChat is clearly on the path to expansion in more international markets.[16]

In addition to integrating on mobile platforms, Tencent is best known for substantial revenue streams from games. QQ, Tencent's flagship product, is much more diversified in terms of how it makes money relative to other social media companies in other markets. The company made $879 million in gaming alone in the second quarter of 2012.[17] Tencent's gaming innovations are rapidly becoming the core of the company's global expansion strategy. Tencent already has four games with active users on Facebook, for instance, with a total user base exceeding 1 million.[18] Recent acquisitions are also part of the mix, with the company acquiring or taking significant equity positions in successful gaming companies Riot Games and Epic Games.[19]

As a social media company, Tencent has develop a far more robust, diversified business of Internet-based services than other social media companies have. Advertising, the primary revenue stream for companies like Google and Facebook, is responsible for just 7 percent of Tencent's total revenue. Tencent's strategy comprises different revenue streams and business models that can be replicated in other markets.

Multichannel Innovation

The fast evolution of China's retail market suggests advances in multichannel retailing as another area of innovation on the horizon. The emerging retail model in China will be based on multichannel capabilities. At some point, this model will result in excess retail capacity in the market as every retailer chases a multichannel capability and market leadership. Not every retailer will make it. This competitive process will no doubt produce new capabilities and change the way we think of an overarching brand that provides goods through a multiple channels.

China's burgeoning consumer class has created an innovation laboratory. The country's market size has justified a new round of product localization supported by in-country, specialized R&D and marketing assets. Its faster pace produces faster innovation cycles. As the multinational focus turns to China first, it is discovering that the outputs of its China-based innovations are finding opportunities in other markets. Companies are developing the capability to rapidly export Chinese-based innovations to other growth markets.

Developed markets are involved as well. The economies of Western Europe and the United States are forecasted to be in a state of slow-growth austerity for the foreseeable future. Household incomes are falling, and consumers in these markets are focused on retrenching and paying off debt. These changing dynamics create new market opportunities that are increasingly born in China and exported elsewhere, the output of China's new export machine.

Notes

1. C. K. Prahalad, *The Fortune at the Bottom of the Pyramid: Eradicating Poverty through Profits* (Philadelphia: Wharton School, 2004).

2. At the time of this writing, Kraft Foods was in the midst of splitting into two entities: Kraft Foods, with a focus on North America, and Mondelez International. In this book I am referring to the company under its original name.

3. Robert Smith, "Rethinking the Oreo for Chinese Consumers," *Planet Money* blog, NPR, January 27, 2012.

4. Laurie Burkitt, "Kraft Craves More of China's Snack Market," *Wall Street Journal*, May 29, 2012.

5. Melanie Lee, "Chinese Drink Joins Coca-Cola's Roster of 'Billion Dollar Brands'," *Globe and Mail*, August 24, 2012.

6. "The World Turned Upside Down," *Economist*, April 15, 2010.

7. Stephen Castle, "O.E.C. Finds New Signs of Weakness in World Economy," *New York Times*, September 13, 2012.

8. Gordon Orr, "Unleashing Innovation in China," McKinsey & Company, January 2011, www.mckinseyquarterly.com/Unleashing_innovation_in_China_2725.

9. Stefan Wagstyl, "Innovation: Replicators No More," *Financial Times*, January 5, 2011.

10. "Vijay Govindarajan Pins Future Growth on Reverse Innovation," *Wall Street Journal*, http://online.wsj.com/ad/article/wbf-govindarajan.

11. "Asian Innovation: Frugal Ideas are Spreading from East to West," *Economist*, March 24, 2012.

12. Maija Palmer, "Tesco Trials UK's First Virtual Store," *Financial Times*, August 6, 2012.

13. David Streitfeld, "Amazon, Forced to Collect a Tax, Is Adding Roots," *New York Times*, September 11, 2012.

14. Internet World Stats, Top 20 Internet Countries by Users—2012 Q2, www.internetworldstats.com/top20.htm.

15. Paul Mozur, "What China Can Teach Facebook," *Wall Street Journal*, May 18, 2012, http://blogs.wsj.com/chinarealtime/2012/05/18/what-china-can-teach-facebook.

16. Josh Ong, "WeChat Messaging Sees Huge Adoption outside China," Next Web, October 12, 2012, http://thenextweb.com/asia/2012/10/12/200-million-users-strong-tencents-wechat-messaging-sees-huge-adoption-outside-of-china.

17. Peter Pham, "Tencent's Assault on Online Gaming," Seeking Alpha, September 10, 2012, http://seekingalpha.com/article/857171-tencent-s-assault-on-online-gaming.

18. Steven Millward, "A Well-Kept Secret: China's Tencent Has Games on Facebook, Doing Well," Tech in Asia, August 2012, www.techinasia.com/tencent-america-icebreak-games-on-facebook.

19. Dean Takahashi, "China's Tencent Marches to the West in Search of Kick-Ass Games," Venture Beat, July 19, 2012, http://venturebeat.com/2012/07/19/chinas-tencent-marches-to-the-west-in-search-of-kick-ass-games-interviews.

CHAPTER 11

The Path Forward

In 2001, Jim O'Neill became the sole head of Goldman Sachs's economic research team. With an ambition to make his mark, Mr. O'Neill started searching for new trends—a new way to frame the global economy that would burnish the reputation of him and his team. The outcome of that search was a new acronym that would begin to pervade corporate vocabulary over the next decade. In a paper published in 2002, the acronym BRIC was born. Now known to many, the acronym stands for Brazil, Russia, India, and China, the four countries that Mr. O'Neill believed would begin to dominate discussions and strategies for economic growth.

Two years later, in a follow-up paper, Mr. O'Neill estimated that GDP from BRIC countries would overtake the established world's economies by 2037. His comparison was the G7, the countries that together represent the globe's current dominant economic powers. After the follow-up paper was published, the label stuck, and business executives started looking at the world quite differently.[1]

Around the same time, a new generation of leaders in China emerged. The protégés of Deng Xiaoping—men like Zhu Rongji and Zhang Xiamen—had held power in China and had mostly continued Deng's legacy, which lifted hundreds of millions out of poverty through an export-led economy. In 2002, Hu Jintao assumed power as China's president. He was the first Chinese president since the 1949 Communist revolution to not have direct ties to it. Like his immediate predecessors, he was a technocrat. Because he was not bound to party orthodoxy, many believed he would usher in a phase of reforms.

In Hu Jintao's years as president (2002–2012), the economy continued its voracious growth, with GDP more than doubling during his tenure. His continued focus on economic growth was representative of the grand bargain between the ruling Communist Party and those they ruled. The grand bargain is a simple one, represented as an implied social contract whereby steady economic growth and standard of living improvements will allow the party to rule unopposed. Holding the grand bargain in place, Hu Jintao's years in power saw little in the area of outright political reform.

Yet forces beyond the party's control have made China's people freer than ever. Rising incomes result in more choices. The pervasive rise of social media has led to a higher level of free expression than people could have imagined. Indeed, China is a much different place from what it was when it became a member of the BRIC club. Its people are freer, and in 10 years the country leapfrogged over the hurdles of multigenerational progress in infrastructure, education, and income growth.

Challenges at a Crossroad

Rapid advances have come with a host of challenges acting as cultural and political headwinds. Rapid economic growth has been a key driver in the rise of protests by the citizenry. Thousands of protests take place every year, at an increasing pace. To fuel economic growth and government-led investment, people's homes and land are taken over by the government. No one really holds legal ownership of his or her property, so people are left with little choice in the matter. The food safety crisis has left many wondering about the trade-off between monetary rewards and overall quality of life. So too do the rising pollution levels. With China's reliance on coal to fuel urbanization and industry, most of its cities are filled with smog beyond any reasonable healthy standard.

Perhaps the greatest sense of unease with the population of China has been the never-ending stain of corruption. Its corrosion appears everywhere, from journalists who present price sheets for favorable coverage to doctors expecting extra payment for services. Provincial bureaucrats are happy to pocket the difference between meager compensation and larger tax revenues derived from land sales that convert rural farmland to skyscrapers and industrial usage.

One of the highest-profile cases of corruption was that of Bo Xilai, the Communist Party's leader in Chongqing, who is now facing life in prison. Under his tenure, Chongqing benefited substantially from the westward march of economic expansion and became one of the fastest growing regions in the country. Yet it also become clear that Bo Xilai practiced much corruption.

With the changes in Chinese society in the past decade, these practices are now public and embarrassing to the governing party. Whereas once these practices would never have seen the light of day, they now threaten the implied contract between the political party and its people and deepen the sense of instability in the country's foundations.

After a generation of incredible economic success, these factors have left many wondering whether the price they have paid for this success is a mortgage on their future quality of life. Many Chinese citizens are starting to vote with their feet. Just as the country's economy demands more skills, China is losing professionals in record numbers because they are choosing to emigrate to other countries. Such emigration has increased 45 percent since 2000, an unprecedented rate. Now an estimated 800,000 Chinese citizens are working abroad, compared with just 60,000 in 1990.[2]

The majority of the 60,000 who emigrated a generation ago did so after the crackdown on the Tiananmen Square uprising. After the crackdown, governments around the world temporarily liberalized their immigration policies toward the Chinese, and a brain drain was the result. As the government crackdown extended beyond the protest, many feared a return to the past. For that generation, the possibility of exile to rural labor camps or of forced public confessions was not an abstract idea. With those fears, many of the nation's best and brightest who had the opportunity to move abroad, primarily through academic study, did so.

At the time, the option to emigrate was only for a select few. Now a new wave of emigration is underway, spurred by a new set of fears. This time, the wave is broader and deeper because more professional people have the resources they need to forge a path elsewhere. The trend might only be a start, because 60 percent of wealthy Chinese reported in a survey to be planning to emigrate.[3]

It's true that many Westerners, including Chinese natives who originally emigrated to the West for education, are coming back, but they are coming back with U.S. and European passports. They are the human equivalent of fast money. With few roots in the country, these people can turn around and take flight, literally, at a moment's notice.

People with a lot of resources are also responding to all of these concerns with their money. More money than ever before is leaving the country—illegally, in most cases. Recent studies show that more businesses are keeping more of their money outside China and that wealthy Chinese individuals are moving and investing more of their assets abroad. Many consider it a hedge against what they perceive to be rising risks to the country's long-term viability.

These trends are more indicative of the challenges associated with a democratic, developed country than with China. Attracting and retaining highly skilled labor through quality of life is an important contribution that governments make in a global economy. Just as financial capital, seeking the highest financial return, moves anywhere around the globe, so too does labor that is highly skilled and scarce move to places that offer the highest "life return." Just when China's government is aiming to move into more sophisticated industries, many of the people it needs to effect this transition are moving out. These people have decided they can exchange their skills for a better environment, more freedom, a larger family, and a system of law that better protects their assets and their workplaces.

China is transitioning from a low-wage manufacturing economy not only to a consumer-led economy but also to a knowledge-based services economy. At this juncture, there are risks. But the country has been at critical junctures before, and economic life continued to prosper. Some of these issues, like corruption, were never really confronted, however. Increasingly, as the society becomes more open, the party may feel more compelled and required to do so. It will have that opportunity with a transition of power and a new leader.

Final Thoughts on Strategy

As we reach the conclusion of this book, the following additional considerations are offered as you start to apply the facts and trends outlined in this book.

Pick Your Spots

Companies will probably have to invest more than they initially planned in order to successfully execute regional expansion strategies. As the retail model evolves to multichannel, and dense, urban distribution networks become more of the norm, large investments will be required to keep pace in a company's chosen markets. There will simply be too many initiatives, too many things to do, that will cost too much if a company tries to be everywhere in the market all at once. Prioritization is critical.

Invest in the Online Space

A company's strategy for playing in China's online world comprises many choices and much complexity. Does it distribute goods through leading ecommerce providers? How does it set up its own presence? What's the best social network to align with to reach the company's target consumers? There is no one correct set of answers, and every company will be different. The choice is clear, though, especially considering the characteristics of China's online population, that participation is required.

Take a Portfolio-Based Distribution Approach

Distribution capability has come a long way in China in the past decade through infrastructure improvements and economic liberalization. Yet as outlined in Chapter 7, inland markets are still far removed from a consolidated, sophisticated distribution capability. The leaders in this space will continue to experiment and use multiple paths toward success. This probably means working with national distributors to supply goods in large, targeted, urban markets. It also means partnering with domestic distributors for access to key relationships, niche markets, and rural areas, if necessary.

Push the Information Advantage

Syndicated data, software, and social media now offer more sources of direct consumer information than ever before. It's not perfect, but it is improving every day as these companies expand themselves and develop better collection methods. Luxury-branded companies currently analyze many of the point-of-sale transactions in their stores to monitor demand and purchasing behavior, which is a beginning. Some may believe that tapping consumer data is premature in a market with such high growth rates in retail, with many struggling with the distribution challenges to get products to the shelf. But the high growth rates mask the intense competition and crowded market in which everyone is going after the same consumer. Knowing more about the consumer will help any company know how to prioritize its resources better, which in the end will win the day.

Understand That Trust and Security Are a Price Premium

Product quality, safety, and consistency lie at the heart of the consumer value proposition in today's market. Emphasize control and visibility across your company's manufacturing and distribution channel (that is, as long as your company can back up the claims). Doing so will enable and help create a price premium in the market.

Make No Presumptions about Pricing

Companies like Starbucks and Apple have shown that high prices are no barrier to broad consumer penetration. Price points above those in developed markets have repeatedly been taken to market and accepted by consumers. Do the research and find out where the consumer price points lie for your company's products. Don't start with any presumptions on how pricing has worked in other markets.

Foster Multilevel Government Relationships

If recent history has taught us anything about relationships with Chinese government officials, it is that these government officials' influence and authority can change rapidly. With the 2012 change in leadership of the governing party, we can expect more change at all levels of government administration.

Furthermore, success in consumer markets today, from a government relations perspective, relies just as much, if not more, on relationships at the local level. Any large company with the resources to invest in government relations should develop the best practices outlined in *Operation China: From Strategy to Execution*, authored by consultants from McKinsey & Company. These best practices include an articulated government engagement plan tied to business objectives at each level of government administration: central, provincial, and municipal.[4]

Remember That Human Resources Are Vital

In the coastal provinces, large labor shortages have been a reality for at least a few years. The market is legendary for high rates of turnover, as employees job-hop frequently. Sectors such as high technology simply cannot find people with the right skills. Some companies have responded by decreasing their training budgets, taking the view that training is a wasted investment if the employees are only going to move on once new skills are acquired. Other companies are showing that these challenges can be overcome. Emphasizing your company's human capital strategy is an important recognition of the challenges unique to this market.

Conclusion

During the time this book was being written, the global economy continued its sluggish recovery from the global recession that began in 2007. Uncertainty about the pace of recovery was pervasive in the United States, specifically in terms of when the moribund labor market would begin to recover. In Europe, it seemed that one currency and sovereign debt crisis led to a resolution plan only to be followed by yet another crisis. Fears of not only a slow and prolonged recovery but also of another recession were always present.

Then China began to slow down. China watchers tried to parse government-released economic data for signs of slowing growth and the risks of an economic hard landing. As the economy began to slow down, goods piled up. Fears increased under the banner headline that a Chinese slowdown would ignite a new global recession. Critics of the Chinese economy came to the forefront, arguing that the economy's continued reliance on exports was detrimental. The reliance on government investment created a huge excess capacity that undermined economic growth. Journalists snapped pictures of fields full of unused steel—graveyards of misspent investment. These were the headlines during the summer of 2012.

But a glimmer of hope—more than a glimmer, actually—arrived in the fall of 2012 when the Chinese government released revised economic growth figures. In the aggregate, the news was good: economic growth was starting to return amid great challenge. The figures showed the dramatic effects of the global slowdown. In 2009, investment accounted for more than 80 percent of GDP, delivered through the largest government stimulus the world has ever seen. At the time, this balanced out the negative export growth of more than 35 percent. The bottom did indeed fall out. Since then, investment has fallen back, and exports have shown continued poor performance.

What's more fascinating, and a sign of great hope for the global economy, is the continued rise in consumption, which is now at its highest percentage of GDP in a decade. Consumer spending was the major contributor to China's economic growth for all of 2011 and through the third quarter of 2012. More than investment, and more than the sad state of exports, consumption has been the leading contributor to economic growth.[5]

In these times, economic uncertainty still exists. Not many have the confidence to simply project the past onto the near future and conclude that the Chinese consumer will continue to lead the way. Yet the latest figures certainly suggest that the long-term picture is just that. China is farther down the path toward a consumer-driven economy than many realized. That unanticipated acceleration provides growth opportunities and, most likely, a continued fast, competitive pace to seize it.

This book has explored the drivers of that transition. An emerging middle class, rapid urbanization, and improved infrastructure have created new growth markets across the entire country. This book has also outlined the segmentation of this growing market, providing insight on those areas of the country where the next large pockets of consumer demand will occur. This analysis has included the key aspects of how goods are marketed and delivered to consumers, the channels of modern retail, distribution trends and challenges, and the unique aspects of China's online world.

Perhaps the most important lesson I have learned in researching and writing this book is the importance of creating a "test and learn" organization. Executives overseeing the Chinese market have told me that improvisation is a frequent and important aspect of their work and the teams they lead. "Let's get in a room and just figure it out" is often the cry. Products are launched in faster cycles in this market. Distribution challenges are overcome through experimentation and resourcefulness. The ability to innovate on the fly and not rely on established, sequential company processes can be a competitive advantage. The resilience to learn from trial and error and respond quickly may be the most important ingredient for success.

Notes

1. Beth Kowitt, "For Mr. BRIC, Nations Meeting a Milestone," *Money*, CNN, June 17, 2009, http://money.cnn.com/2009/06/17/news/economy/goldman_sachs_jim_oneill_interview.fortune.

2. Ian Johnson, "Wary of Future, Professionals Leave China in Record Numbers," *New York Times*, October 31, 2012.

3. Shi Jing and Yu Ran, "Chinese Rich Are Keen to Emigrate," *China Daily USA*, November 11, 2011, http://usa.chinadaily.com.cn/business/2011-11/03/content_14028392.htm.

4. Jimmy Hexter and Jonathan Woetzel, *Operation China: From Strategy to Execution* (Cambridge, MA: Harvard Business School Press, 2007).

5. "China's Consumer-Led Growth," *Economist*, October 20, 2012, www.economist.com/blogs/freeexchange/2012/10/rebalancing-china.

About the Author

Dave M. Holloman is currently an associate partner with IBM's Global Business Services organization. He advises clients on the intersection of business strategy and technology to maximize the value of enterprise technology. He also designs and leads large-scale, broad-based business transformations focused on the areas of go-to-market strategy, supply chain, analytics, and innovation. Dave has more than 20 years of global experience in applying technology and leading practices to help companies develop new sources of competitive advantage.

His career has included executive and leadership positions in the world's leading technology companies as well as in entrepreneurial start-ups, professional services, product management, and product marketing roles. He has repeatedly formed and led high-performance organizations toward higher growth in newly developing markets.

Dave has received certification in production and inventory management from the American Production and Inventory Control Society. He received a B.S. in industrial engineering from the University of Cincinnati and an M.B.A. from the J. L. Kellogg Graduate School of Management at Northwestern University in Chicago.

Dave lives in Chicago with his wife and two children. He enjoys skiing with his family as well as taking an occasional backpacking trip.

Index

Page numbers followed by *f* indicates figures and *t* indicates tables